W9-COJ-765

Joint
REPLACEMENTS

ABDO
Publishing Company

Joint REPLACEMENTS

by Leslie Galliker

Content Consultant

Dr. John D. DesJardins

Assistant Professor of Bioengineering

Clemson University

Credits

Published by ABDO Publishing Company, PO Box 398166, Minneapolis, MN 55439. Copyright © 2014 by Abdo Consulting Group, Inc. International copyrights reserved in all countries. No part of this book may be reproduced in any form without written permission from the publisher. The Essential Library™ is a trademark and logo of ABDO Publishing Company.

Printed in the United States of America,
North Mankato, Minnesota
062013
092013

 THIS BOOK CONTAINS AT LEAST 10% RECYCLED MATERIALS.

Editor: Arnold Ringstad
Series Designer: Craig Hinton

Photo credits: Sebastian Kaulitzki/Shutterstock Images, cover, 45; CLIPAREA | Custom media/Shutterstock Images, cover; Shutterstock Images, cover, 48; Wellcome Trust Library/Custom Medical Stock Photo, 7; Lori Ann Cook-Neisler, The Pantagraph/AP Images, 10; Susan Leggett/Shutterstock Images, 12; iStockphoto/Thinkstock, 15; Digital Vision/Thinkstock, 17; Alila Medical Images/Shutterstock Images, 20, 31, 37; Bernd Weissbrod/picture-alliance/dpa/AP Images, 22; CCN/BSIP/SuperStock, 25; Monkey Business Images/Shutterstock Images, 27; VR Photos/Shutterstock Images, 28; imagebroker.net/SuperStock, 34; Tom Gannam/AP Images, 40; Michael Mitchell/Shutterstock Images, 43; St. Petersburg Times/ZUMA Press/Newscom, 51; Kevin Nortz/The Herald/AP Images, 53; Mark Elias/AP Images, 55; Kzenon/Shutterstock Images, 57; Dave Souza/The Herald News/AP Images, 60, 80; ARENA Creative/Shutterstock Images, 63; MedicImage/Universal Images Group/Getty Images, 65; Charlie Riedel/AP Images, 69; Steve Reed/Shutterstock Images, 70; Lannis Waters/ZUMA Press/Newscom, 73; Mike Hutmacher KRT/Newscom, 74; Jodi Jacobson/E+/Getty Images, 77; BSIP/UIG/Getty Images, 83, 87; Jahi Chikwendiu/The Washington Post/Getty Images, 89; Science Photo Library/Custom Medical Stock Photo, 91; Will Vragovic/ZUMA Press/Newscom, 92; Tony Avelar/Christian Science Monitor/Getty Images, 95; Torin Halsey, Wichita Falls Times Record News/AP Images, 99

Library of Congress Control Number: 2013932974

Cataloging-in-Publication Data

Galliker, Leslie.
 Joint replacements / Leslie Galliker.
  p. cm. -- (Medical marvels)
Includes bibliographical references and index.
ISBN 978-1-61783-903-0
1. Artificial joints--Juvenile literature. 2. Joint prosthesis--Juvenile literature. 3. Biomechanics--Juvenile literature. I. Title.
617.5--dc23

                                         2013932974

Contents

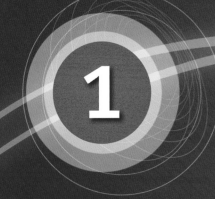
A Girl Who Lived in Pain

Caitlin Ryan wanted to be a dancer, but her dream seemed impossible. When doctors diagnosed her at the age of three with juvenile rheumatoid arthritis (JRA), she was in nearly constant pain. JRA is an autoimmune disease. Among the immune system's targets can be the body's joints, the parts linking bones together. An estimated 300,000 children in the United States have this disease, and Caitlin had the most common form.[1]

JRA is an unpredictable disease, and its causes are unknown. Before doctors determined Caitlin had it, they thought she might have cancer or a muscular disease. Symptoms such as pain, swelling, and stiffness can suddenly flare up all over the body and then disappear just as quickly. There is no known cure.

People with JRA suffer from severe pain in their joints, including the many joints in their hands.

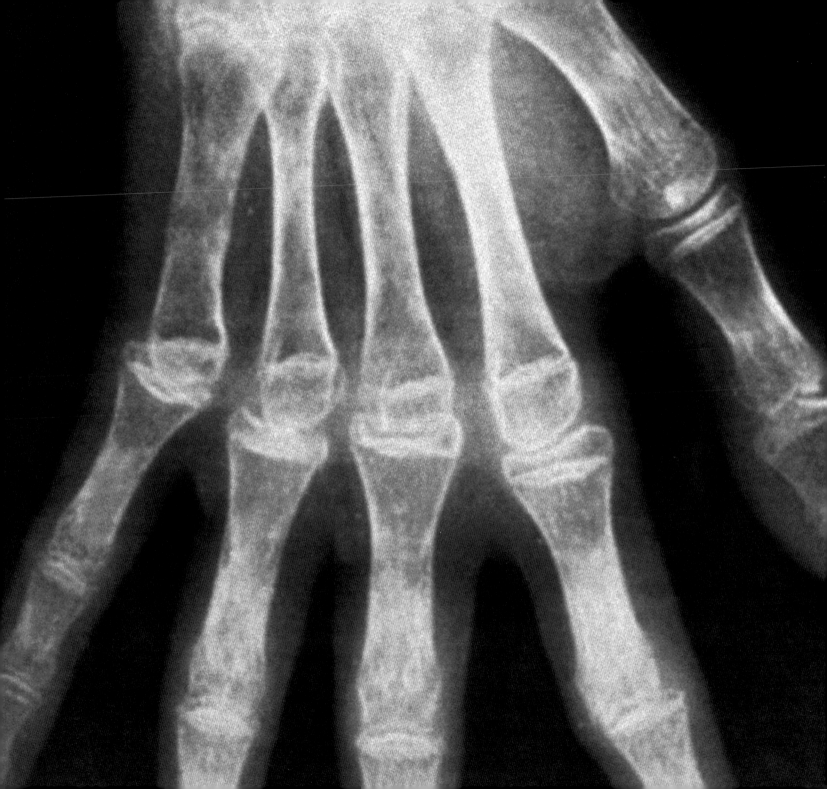

JRA Pain

When asked to explain how she felt each day before her surgery, Caitlin said, "You can feel your joints throbbing like you can feel your heart beat after you run. It feels like your joints are going to pop out." She added, "I've dealt with stuff like my joints hurting and everything hurting most of my life. . . . Once you know that you have it and you can't stop it, you just sort of have to live with it."[3]

Before her surgery, Caitlin often felt anxious and depressed. The pain left her unable to even pick up a pencil. She had trouble sleeping, and the medications her doctor prescribed did not seem to help. Neither did alternative treatments such as acupuncture and massage therapy. No matter where Caitlin and her family turned for relief, nothing seemed to permanently ease the pain. And her condition was worsening.

In the span of one year, measurements and X-rays showed her crumbling hip had shortened her left leg by approximately one inch (2.5 cm). "The bone in the hip," her mother said, "was dying from the damage."[2] There seemed to be no option left but to surgically replace her left hip joint.

The surgery would not be easy. Young patients often face special challenges with joint replacement. Since their bones are so small, it can be difficult to find replacement parts in the correct sizes. They must receive replacement parts especially designed for children. Caitlin's parents worried about their daughter's future development. Joint replacement in children can hinder their bones' ability to grow. Her parents had hoped to wait until she was older to have the surgery, but finally they decided Caitlin had gone through enough pain. In 2009, at age 11, her world changed when she received a left hip replacement.

A New Hip

After her surgery and a period of rehabilitation, Caitlin knew exactly how she wanted to spend her time. "I've never been able to really dance," she said.[4] Soon she was practicing all kinds of dancing, from hip-hop to ballet.

Caitlin's newly replaced left hip worked well. Still, it was important she continue taking medications to keep her disease under control. Her story was an inspiration for other

+ Slowing Growth

Before Caitlin was diagnosed with JRA, she was tall for her age and growing fast. Doctors predicted she would eventually grow to approximately five feet ten inches (178 cm) as an adult. With JRA, her growth slowed to approximately 0.4 inches (1 cm) every two months. Although she may not grow as tall as expected, Caitlin sees this as a minor trade-off for the relief she has found.

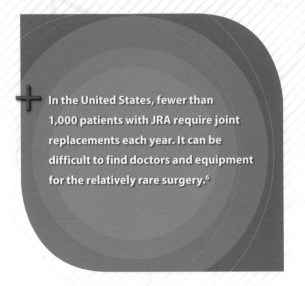

In the United States, fewer than 1,000 patients with JRA require joint replacements each year. It can be difficult to find doctors and equipment for the relatively rare surgery.[6]

kids suffering from JRA, and she was named the 2010 National Arthritis Walk Youth Honoree.

Her left hip felt better, but daily pain still shot through Caitlin's right hip. After experiencing such a dramatic improvement following the left hip replacement, she and her parents knew what had to come next. They realized it was important they waste no time in dealing with it, and in 2010 Caitlin received a right hip replacement. Once again, the surgery was a success.

An Active Life

With her two new hips, Caitlin began living a fuller, more active life. She still needed to take medication, but she found other ways to help relieve her arthritis symptoms. Caitlin loves swimming. She found it relieves pain and is also lots of fun. "Being in the pool feels great," she said.[5] Caitlin had tried playing softball before the surgery, but her condition meant she could not participate fully. Before the surgery, she explained, "I had to have someone run for me."[7] Now, she could run for herself. Caitlin also found

Modern hip replacements make it possible for patients to return to activities such as softball.

pain relief was not just about keeping active. She discovered staying calm and relaxed are helpful ways to control flare-ups.

Some JRA patients must wear leg braces in order to walk normally.

Like many people her age, Caitlin loves to shop. She is also happy curling up and reading a good book; her favorites are the Harry Potter and Twilight series. Listening to music or watching funny TV shows keeps her mind off the pain, Caitlin says.

Whether they are children or adults, joint replacement patients face many challenges as they continue to live their lives. The parts used in the new joint can wear out over time. Because they get the surgery when they are so young, children who get new joints may require a second or even a third replacement surgery during their lifetime. But for people facing severe joint problems, the challenges of replacement surgery are relatively minor obstacles compared with the benefits. Joint replacement surgery has improved the quality of life for millions of people around the world.

When Nothing Else Works

Dr. Mark Figgie, an expert in the field of joint replacement, is looking into ways to improve the procedure for young patients. Figgie sees a need for smaller joint implants to fit smaller skeletal systems as well as a need to treat patients early, before their arthritis worsens. He is working to set up a system for hospitals around the country to share information about joint replacements in children. Because children in need of the surgery are rare, sharing experience from these procedures could enable all hospitals to provide even better care to the few young patients who do require joint replacements.

Joints and Joint Problems

In general, the job of a joint is to connect bones and enable motion. A joint is made up of tissues called ligaments, tendons, and cartilage. These tissues create the connection between bones and make motion possible. They are found all over the body. Two of the joints most critical to everyday movement are the knee and the hip. Because they receive so much wear and tear, they are the most frequently replaced joints in the body. In the knee, three bones connect to allow your joint to bend and twist. The bones are the tibia (the shinbone), the femur (the thighbone), and the patella (the kneecap). Together they form the tibiofemoral and the patellofemoral joints. In the hip, the femur and the pelvis (the hip bone) connect, giving the leg a wide range of motion. The scientific name for the hip joint is the acetabulofemoral joint. Joints are found wherever two or more bones connect. They include the shoulders, elbows, fingers, ankles, and even the tiny bones in the ear.

The knee and hip joints are two of the most critical body parts that make walking and running possible.

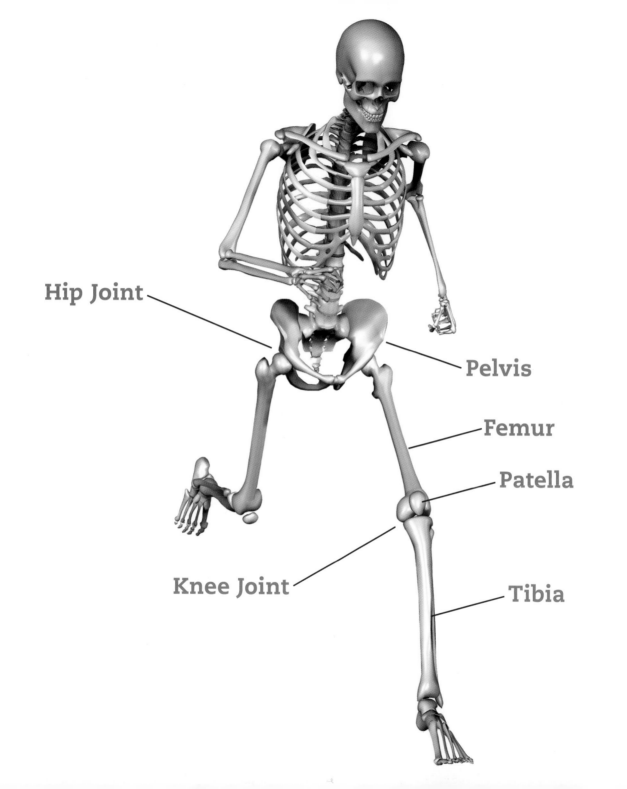

Hip Joint

Pelvis

Femur

Patella

Knee Joint

Tibia

Types and Parts of Joints

Joints are often divided into three major types based on the kind of movement they allow. The first type, known as a fixed joint, allows almost no movement at all. For instance, the connections between the bones of the skull allow the skull to expand as the brain grows but do not permit the bones to move actively. This type of joint is made from fibrous tissue composed mostly of a protein called collagen. Other than in the skull, fixed joints can also be found connecting the bones in the pelvis together and connecting teeth to their sockets in the jaw.

The second type, known as a cartilaginous joint, allows slightly more movement than fixed joints. In this type, a plate of connective tissue called cartilage sits between bones, cushioning the movement between them. The bones of the vertebrae (backbone) have cartilaginous joints between them. Movement in these joints is typically limited to slight bending and twisting.

The third type, known as a synovial joint, allows a much wider range of motion than fixed and

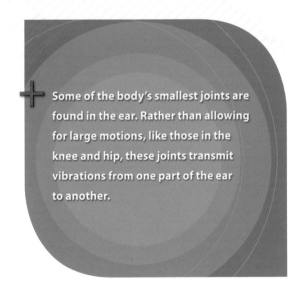

Some of the body's smallest joints are found in the ear. Rather than allowing for large motions, like those in the knee and hip, these joints transmit vibrations from one part of the ear to another.

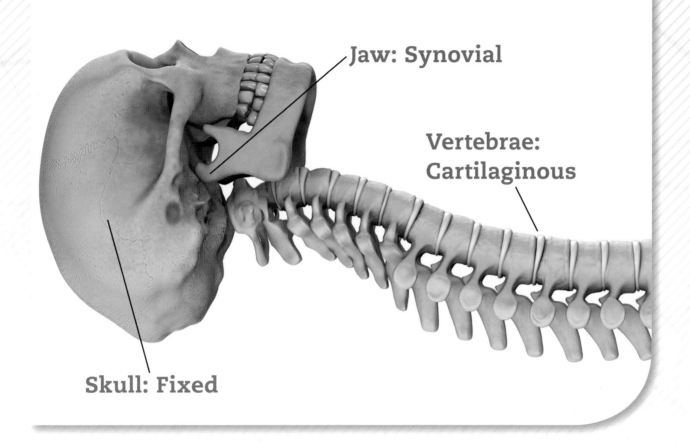

Jaw: Synovial

Vertebrae: Cartilaginous

Skull: Fixed

cartilaginous joints. In these joints, capsules called bursas filled with synovial fluid surround the points of connection between bones. The synovial membrane, which covers the bursas, creates the synovial fluid. The synovial fluid acts like oil in machinery, lubricating the moving parts to prevent damage from friction. During fetal development, the parts of the bursas connected to bones become cartilage, providing additional cushioning to the joint. Synovial joints are the most complicated type of joint, and

Ball-and-Socket Joints

A few of the body's synovial joints are also known as ball-and-socket joints. In these joints, the rounded end of one bone fits into a rounded hole at the end of another. The rounded end can rotate freely within the hole, permitting the widest range of motion of any joints in the body. The shoulder and the hips contain ball-and-socket joints. The wide flexibility and frequent use of these joints means they are among the most susceptible to injuries.

they are the most frequently replaced. They are found all over the body, including in the knee, hip, shoulder, jaw, and fingers.

Several other parts of the body assist joint functions. Ligaments are elastic tissues that hold together bones within the joints. They are tough enough to hold bones together while flexible enough to stretch during active movements. Tendons, the structures that connect muscles to bone, transmit the force generated by the muscle across joints in order to create motion. They also support and stabilize joints. The bones themselves, hard structures consisting of minerals and living cells, provide the framework for the body and the linking points for joints. Their ends, located within joints, are usually covered in cartilage.

Joint Problems

As with any other parts of the body, diseases can affect joints. Other than joint problems caused by physical injuries, the various types of arthritis account for a majority of all joint disease. Arthritis is a disorder involving inflammation of joints. Major types include osteoarthritis, rheumatoid arthritis, ankylosing spondylitis, and psoriatic arthritis.

People suffering from osteoarthritis suffer from a loss of cartilage, resulting in severe pain when bones scrape together without proper cushioning. Osteoarthritis is the most common form of arthritis. Rheumatoid arthritis is marked by inflammation and thickening of synovial membranes, resulting in pain, stiffness, and restriction of movement. It affects women four times more often than men.[1] In ankylosing spondylitis, joints in the bones of the spine and pelvis become inflamed and the bones grow together across the joint. The fusion

+ Arthritis History

Arthritis has been affecting living things since long before human beings were around. Paleontologists have found that some dinosaurs likely suffered from a form of arthritis. Human arthritis is mentioned in writing dating back 6,500 years, but the disease was relatively rare until the 1600s, in part because most people died at a young age. The terms *arthritis* and *rheumatoid arthritis* were coined in the 1800s. Today, an estimated 50 million Americans suffer from a form of arthritis.[2]

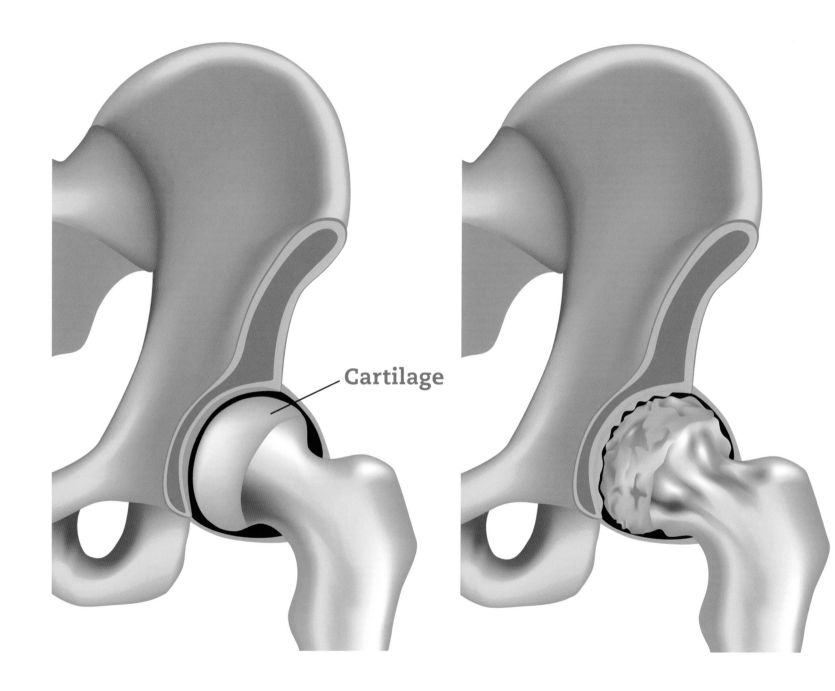
Cartilage

of bones stiffens the spine and leaves the joint unable to move. Psoriatic arthritis is associated with the skin disorder psoriasis. Along with the usual skin redness and irritation brought about by psoriasis, the disease causes joint pain and stiffness, especially in the fingers and toes.

Joint problems can also be caused by physical trauma. For instance, after a serious knee injury, post-traumatic arthritis can occur. Fractures of bones surrounding the knee or tears of knee ligaments may damage cartilage over time and limit the function of the knee. Another cause of joint damage is the use of corticosteroids. These drugs are used for anti-inflammatory purposes in the body, but they can also result in the death of bones, most commonly in the hip. Scientists are unsure how the drugs lead to this damage, which can be severe enough to require a joint replacement.

Diagnosis

Before any kind of treatment begins, and long before joint replacement is considered, a doctor must diagnose a problem in the patient. The doctor will ask about the patient's symptoms and perform a physical examination. Because joint issues can be difficult to decisively diagnose from a simple visual examination, doctors use techniques that allow them to look inside their patients' joints. Three common techniques are X-rays, magnetic resonance imaging (MRI), and computed axial tomography (CAT).

A healthy hip joint, *left*, contains cushioning cartilage. The joint of a person with osteoarthritis, *right*, lacks some of this cushioning.

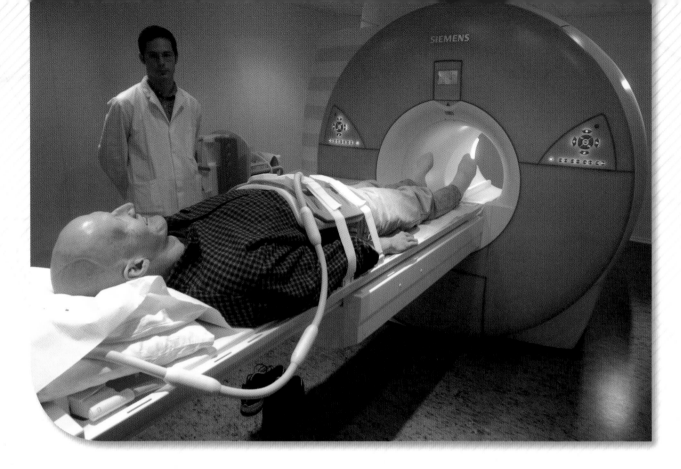

During the MRI scan, the patient lies in a tube containing a powerful electromagnet. When the magnet is turned on, the billions of hydrogen atoms in the patient's body become oriented in the same direction. Then, smaller magnets create magnetic fields near the part of the body to be scanned. By varying their power, the smaller magnets alter the alignment of the hydrogen atoms in that part of the body in the particular way needed for the scan. A scanner detects this magnetic field, and a computer turns that information into an image of structures within the patient. Specialized doctors called radiologists are trained to examine these images to diagnose injuries and swelling in the cartilage, tendons, and ligaments. Because most MRI machines confine patients to a tube, and because the scan can take up to 45 minutes, some people with a fear of enclosed spaces find MRI scans difficult to endure. Newer machines allow patients to stand or lie on a flat table during the procedure.

For CAT scans, X-ray equipment is combined with computers to create images of the inside of the body. Each image is of a thin slice of the patient. By combining these images, the computer can generate three-dimensional views of the body. Some soft tissues, such as ligaments and muscles, show up on CAT scan images, making this examination useful in diagnosing joint problems. After the doctor has gathered this information

MRI Safety and Comfort

During MRI examinations, doctors make every effort to maximize patient comfort and safety. The enormous magnets involved create extremely loud thumping and humming noises, so patients may be offered or may request earplugs or headphones to block some of this noise. MRI scanners are air-conditioned and well lit to help relieve claustrophobia. The most important safety precaution when undergoing an MRI examination is to avoid bringing any kind of metal into the scanner. The powerful magnets could violently pull on things like body piercings, causing harm. For that reason, patients must leave jewelry, pens, keys, and metal eyeglasses behind while being scanned.

> "The vast majority of these joints—80 to 90 percent—are still performing well at 20 years after the surgery. Try to think of something you bought that was still working 20 years later."[3]
>
> *—Surgeon Della Valle on joint replacements*

about the joint, he or she discusses the pros and cons of surgery with the patient. As with any surgery, there are inherent risks involved in joint replacement. The possibility of an infection or other complication always exists. And even if the surgery goes according to plan, recovery can sometimes be a long and painful process. Still, for many patients, the rewards of joint replacement surgery outweigh the risks.

Modern scanning technology can give doctors incredible views of patients' joints.

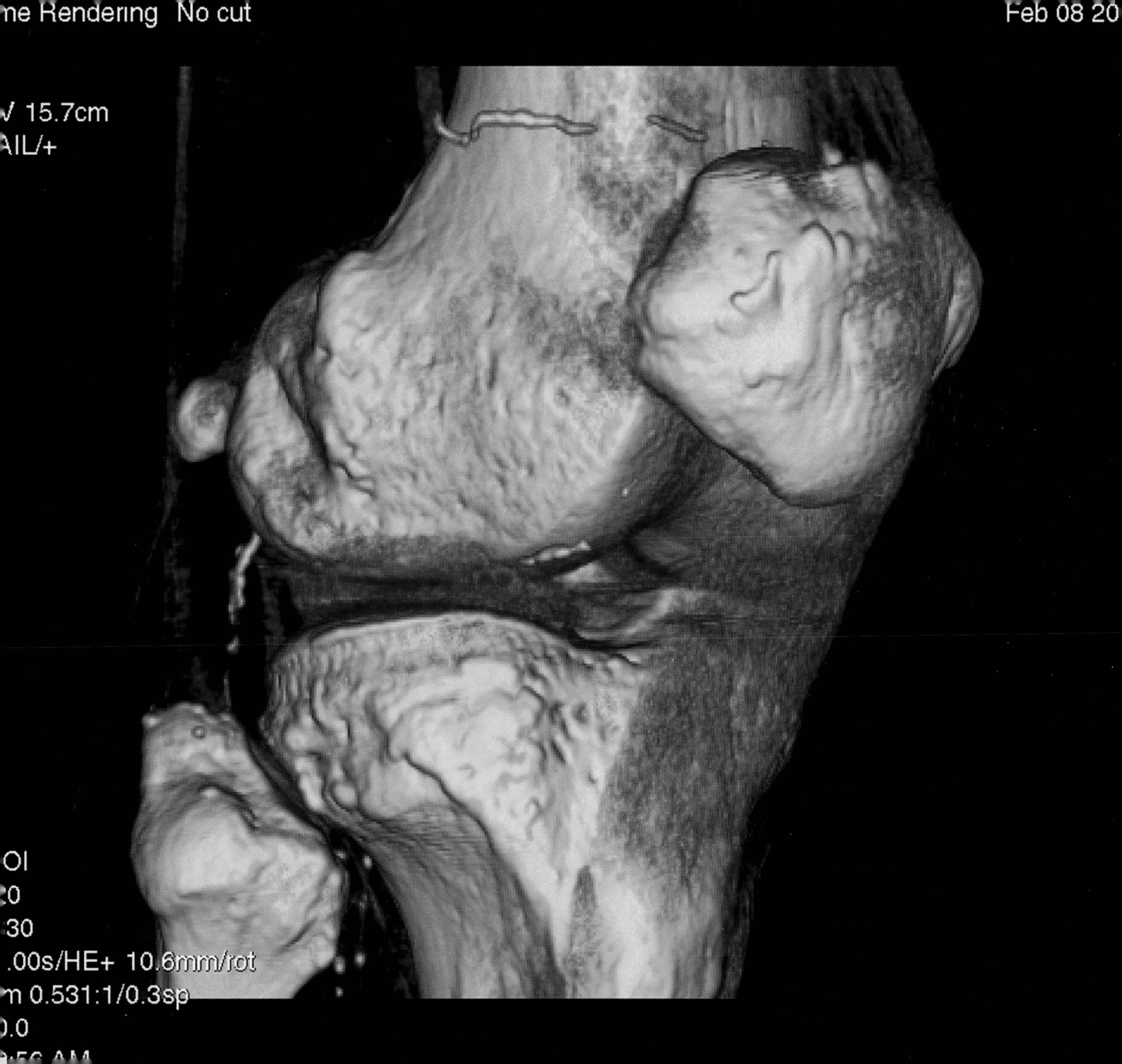

me Rendering No cut
Feb 08 20
15.7cm
AIL/+
OI
30
.00s/HE+ 10.6mm/rot
m 0.531:1/0.3sp

Hip and Knee Replacements

Hips and knees are the most commonly replaced joints, largely because they receive more daily wear and tear than other joints. The earliest indication of a problem with these joints is simple joint pain. The pain usually begins long before a definitive diagnosis and a surgery recommendation. The pain may become so severe the person will try to avoid using the joint. When the muscles around the joint weaken from disuse, using the joint becomes even more difficult.

Although research suggests joint replacements significantly improve long-term health prospects, some people are still anxious about having replacement surgery. One study has shown women appear to delay the surgery more than men, perhaps due to higher pain tolerance or a desire to follow their doctors' orders. According to a physical therapy expert at the University of Delaware,

A visit to the doctor for joint pain is sometimes the first step on the road to joint replacement surgery.

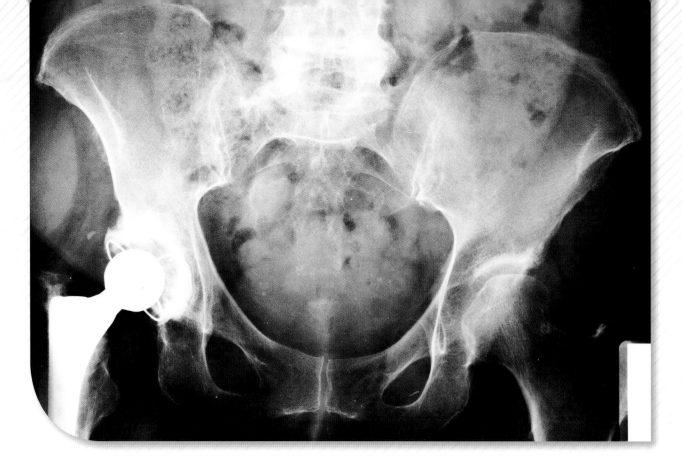

"doctors typically tell patients to wait to have knee replacements until they just can't stand the pain any longer."[1] This advice, which may delay joint replacement surgery, can sometimes lead to worsened outcomes compared with those who get the surgery earlier. This must be balanced, however, by the life expectancy of both the joint replacement and the patient. When a joint replacement is carried out early in life, patients may need one or more additional replacement surgeries as the artificial joints wear out.

The structure of a hip replacement, *left*, mimics the way a natural hip joint, *right*, works.

Hip Replacements

Hip replacements are usually done to relieve severe arthritis pain. During the surgery, doctors replace the ends of the patient's hip bones with artificial components called implants. These components are designed to act like the natural ball-and-socket joint in the body and consist of three parts. The first part, a cup-shaped implant made of plastic, ceramic, or metal, is connected to the pelvis. It acts as the socket in the new joint. The second part is a metal or ceramic ball that fits into the cup. The third part anchors the ball and extends down into the femur to support the new joint.

There are two methods to hold the new joint replacement in place: cemented and uncemented. The patient and doctor must discuss which is best for the patient's particular case. In a cemented replacement, special bone paste is used to connect the implant to existing bone. In an uncemented replacement, the implant's surface is designed to promote bone growth to hold the joint in place. Doctors can also choose to use both types, with one bone connection being cemented and the other being uncemented. Cemented replacements are generally used in older patients, since their bones are frailer. Uncemented replacements are typically used in younger patients whose healthy bones can more easily grow into the implant.

Hip replacement surgery can be done in one of two ways: traditionally or with an arthroscopic procedure. The two methods differ based on the size of the cut into the patient's body. In both types,

Cemented versus Uncemented

In 2010, doctors in Sweden published a study examining the success rates of cemented and uncemented hip replacements. In the study, they looked at the results of more than 170,000 replacements done between 1992 and 2007. They looked only at those patients who received totally cemented or totally uncemented replacements, ignoring those whose hip replacements included both types of components. The doctors discovered that 15 percent of uncemented replacements needed repair within ten years. Only 6 percent of cemented replacements needed repair within that time span.[2]

the surgery begins when the patient receives a general anesthetic, relaxing the muscles and putting the patient to sleep. This keeps the patient from feeling pain during the surgery. In traditional hip replacement, the surgeon makes a large incision on the side of the leg near the hip. In an arthroscopic procedure, one or two small incisions are made. The remaining procedures accomplish the same things, except that in arthroscopic surgery the doctor does not have as much access to the joint and must use miniature cameras and tools to complete each step. Arthroscopic surgery causes less damage to surrounding tissues and can enable a quicker recovery.

After the incisions are made, the surgeon moves muscles out of the way and locates the hip joint. The ball portion of the patient's natural ball-and-socket joint—the upper end of the femur—is sliced off using a bone-cutting tool. More bone is removed in the main part of the femur

Hip replacement surgery generally lasts between one and three hours.

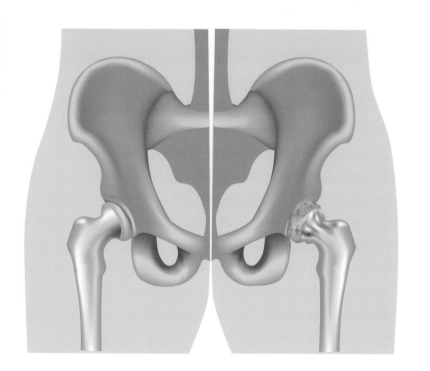

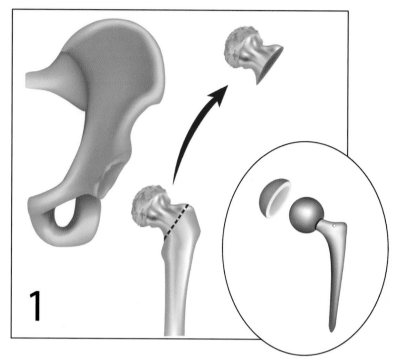

1

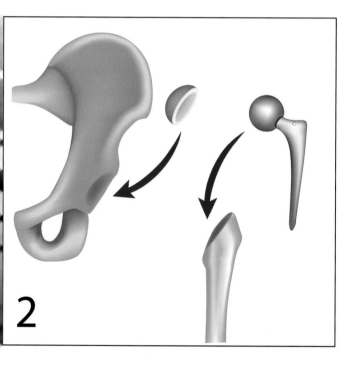

2

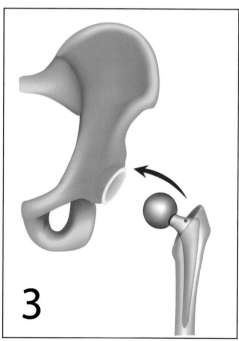

3

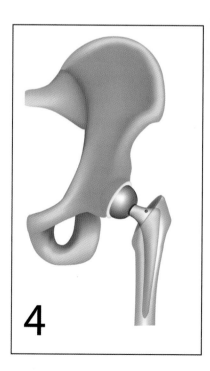

4

to give the stem of the implant a place to attach. Next, the surgeon uses either the cemented or uncemented technique to attach the stem part of the joint to the patient's femur. Once this is in place, the doctor cleans the surface of the existing hip bone. Damaged bone and cartilage are removed in preparation for the attachment of the artificial socket. Again, either the cemented or uncemented method is used to attach it. The artificial ball is attached to the anchor previously installed on the femur and inserted into the socket. Finally, the joint capsule is closed, the thigh muscles are put back in place, and the incision is closed up.

The Development of Hip Replacements

The history of using surgery to solve problems with the hip joint dates back to the early 1800s. At that time, joint problems were frequently solved by simply amputating the entire limb. Joint removal and replacement can be time consuming, and in an age without effective general anesthesia, the quickness of a surgery was extremely important. In the 1820s, some surgeons experimented with removing parts of the hip joint. The pain relief was effective, but patients lacked stability and mobility.

The first artificial hip joints were developed in the late 1800s. One surgeon experimented with ivory, nickel, and plaster. Work continued into the early 1900s, but patients continued to have to sacrifice stability and mobility for their pain relief. In 1938, British doctor Phillip Wiles designed a stainless steel artificial hip but was ultimately unsuccessful in solving the ongoing issues with hip replacement surgeries. During the 1940s, Kenneth McKee, who had trained with Wiles, experimented with cementing techniques. He patented a hip replacement device in 1951, but it was prone to loosening and mechanical failure.

British surgeon John Charnley is considered by many to be the pioneer of total hip replacement. Charnley had been working toward this goal for years before he achieved success. In 1959, he delivered a speech suggesting contemporary surgeons were not well equipped to conduct full joint replacement surgeries: "This type of surgery demands training in mechanical techniques which, though elementary in practical engineering, are as yet unknown in the training of a surgeon."[3] He finally developed a successful implant in 1962. His device combined metal and a material known as Teflon, later replaced by a material called

Teflon

Teflon is one company's brand name for a material called polytetrafluoroethylene (PTFE). It was invented by accident by a US scientist in 1938. He noticed a container of tetrafluoroethylene gas, used as a coolant, still had some weight in it even though the gas had stopped flowing. Opening the container, he found a white, slippery material had coated the inside. Because of this slipperiness and the fact that it does not react with other chemicals, PTFE is widely used as a nonstick coating for cooking. These qualities also made it attractive for initial use in joint replacements.

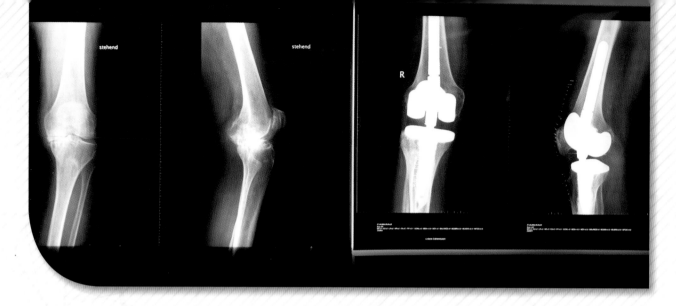

polyethylene. The device, initially used in the elderly, inactive population, proved to be the basis for all subsequent implants.

Charnley made considerable efforts to improve his device as new information came in. He even wrote to his patients asking them if he could have the artificial hips back after they died. As one of his colleagues remembered, most of his patients were so satisfied with the hip they complied with his request: "If someone died, we would be sent to go and collect the hips and the lymph nodes to correlate the facts and to see how the joints had worked during the 13 or 20 years they had been in the body."[3] Using this information, Charnley and other researchers continued refining the artificial hip's design.

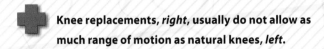

Knee Replacements

The knee joint, like the hip, is a synovial joint. However, it does not use the ball-and-socket mechanism found in the hip and shoulder. Instead, it is a pivotal hinge joint, allowing the leg to bend in two directions and rotate slightly. As with hip replacement, knee replacement is done to relieve pain resulting from arthritis. Implants for knee replacement are typically made of metal and plastic. Modern designs allow patients not only to bend their knee, but also to make the slight rotations healthy knees are capable of. Cemented and uncemented knee replacements have similar pros and cons as do hip replacements.

Before surgery, the patient is put to sleep using a general anesthetic. A long incision is made from just above the knee to just below it. After moving muscles, tendons, and ligaments out of the way, the ends of the femur, the tibia, and optionally the patella are cleaned and damaged cartilage is removed. The surgeon then attaches the artificial joint parts to these three bones, using either the cemented or uncemented method. Next, the parts are connected, forming the completed artificial knee. Muscles,

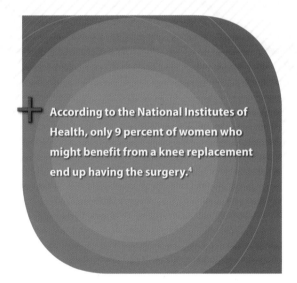

According to the National Institutes of Health, only 9 percent of women who might benefit from a knee replacement end up having the surgery.[4]

tendons, and ligaments are returned to their original places, and the surgeon closes up the joint capsule and the incision. Arthroscopic methods are a recent development. More and more surgeons are performing them. Studies are underway to determine whether the arthroscopic surgery improves outcomes for knee replacement patients over the regular method. A few specialty hospitals even use robots to assist with hip and knee surgery in an effort to increase the accuracy and reliability of the procedure.

Knee Replacement History

The history of surgery used to relieve knee joint pain dates back to the 1860s. At that time, surgeon A. B. J. Ferguson invented a technique for removing damaged bone from the joint and inserting cushioning material between the tibia and the femur. Doctors tried using a wide assortment of cushioning materials, including skin, muscle,

Knees Outnumber Hips

Although the hip was the first joint to be replaced, knee replacement surgeries are now more common than hip replacements. Approximately 600,000 total knee replacements are performed each year in the United States.[5] Approximately 285,000 total hip replacements are performed each year.[6] Hip replacements are generally more expensive. Knee replacements cost approximately $45,000, while hip replacements can cost up to $100,000.[7]

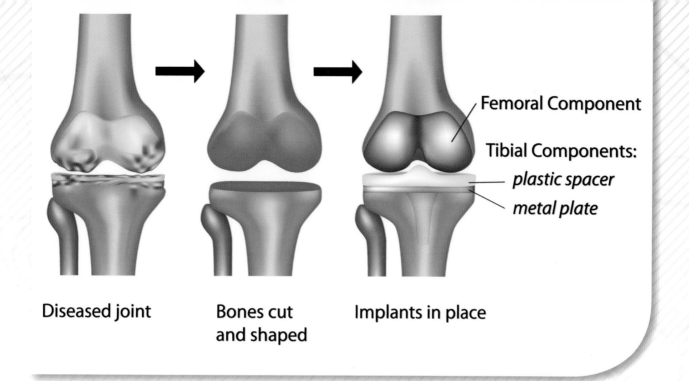

Diseased joint

Bones cut and shaped

Implants in place

Femoral Component

Tibial Components:
plastic spacer
metal plate

and even pig bladders. It was not until the 1940s that surgeons began actually replacing parts of the knee. Similar advances taking place in hip replacement surgery inspired the knee surgeons of the time. In early knee procedures, a metal or plastic implant replaced the surface of either the tibia or the femur. Issues with loosening and pain plagued these early attempts at replacing parts of the knee joint.

Studies done in the late 1940s and early 1950s confirmed the poor quality of these early knee surgeries. In a 1949 study conducted at a hospital in Memphis, Tennessee, nearly 30 percent of these procedures had outcomes rated as either "poor" or "failure." Another study conducted in an Iowa

Knee Replacement Statistics

Years	1991–1994	1995–1998	1999–2002	2003–2006	2007–2010
Patients	431,050	530,128	578,614	816,497	915,562
Average Age	73.8	74.5	74.7	74.7	74.2[9]

hospital showed nearly half of the surgeries rated as "failures."[8] A 1954 article by doctor L. G. P. Shiers brought up this poor track record and made several recommendations about the future of knee replacement. He identified three key problems that a knee replacement would have to solve. First, patients would need to be able to flex their knee joint back and forth. Second, the extension of the joint would need to be limited to 180 degrees. Finally, the artificial joint would need to keep the knee stable during side-to-side motion. Shiers included images of his implant as well as a description of the surgical procedure it would require. His paper laid the groundwork for an explosion of artificial knee development in the subsequent decades.

In the 1950s, doctors developed the first full knee replacements. Designed as simple hinges, the replacements proved too weak for everyday use. When they became loose, they caused knee pain. In 1968, Canadian surgeon Frank Gunston developed the first knee replacement that took into account not only the knee joint's hinge action but also its rotation and gliding motions. Gunston refused to patent his invention, wanting it to help as many people as possible without restrictions. This decision meant other researchers were able to build from his design. Gunston's knee replacement became the basis for subsequent refinements in artificial knee joint technology. However, his implants were still not perfect. Loosening, usually stemming from a poor connection between the implant and the patient's bones, was still a major problem.

New developments in the 1970s led to the mobile-bearing knee replacement. This technology allowed the parts of the artificial knee to move more freely, giving the patient a greater and more natural range of motion. However, the mobile-bearing design also requires strong ligaments in the knee to hold it steady, meaning it is usually recommended only for younger patients.

Resurfacing

Full joint replacement is sometimes unnecessary for young patients suffering from arthritis. These patients may benefit from a simpler procedure called joint resurfacing. In resurfacing, only the damaged surface of the joint is removed. In hip resurfacing, for instance, the head of the femur is kept intact rather than being cut off and replaced. It is trimmed, and a covering is installed to provide a smooth, undamaged surface. As with a full replacement, the socket in the hip bone can be replaced entirely, and a smooth, new shell can be inserted. Resurfacing can also be done in the knee joint.

Resurfacing procedures can give patients more mobility and a decreased risk of dislocation. It is also easier to carry out a revision surgery for a resurfacing compared with a full replacement. Finally, if the patient later needs a full joint replacement, it is relatively simple to convert the resurfacing into a replacement. However, there are also a few downsides to resurfacing. In hip resurfacing, if the head of the femur is damaged but not replaced, this part of the bone can later become fractured. If this happens, the patient will end up needing a full hip replacement. Additionally, resurfacing is usually a more difficult operation than replacement, and a larger incision is needed to carry out the procedure.

A doctor holds a traditional hip implant, *left,* **and an implant used in a new resurfacing technique,** *right.*

Other Types of Joint Replacements

Most joint replacement surgeries are done on hips and knees, but replacements can also help people suffering from problems in their shoulders, fingers, ankles, and elbows. Perhaps because the shoulder is so commonly used in daily life, its complexity is not often appreciated. When shoulder pain strikes, however, doctors have the tools to replace the joint. When shoulder replacement surgery was originally developed in the 1950s, it was performed mainly to treat severe fractures. Today, the procedure can also be done to relieve severe arthritis pain.

The shoulder is made up of three bones. The first is the humerus (the upper arm bone). The second is the scapula (the shoulder blade). The third is the clavicle (the collarbone). Like the hip joint, the shoulder is a ball-and-socket joint, allowing for a wide range of motion. The ball shape at the end

Many sports and activities can put severe strain on shoulders over time, sometimes leading to the necessity of a joint replacement later in life.

Shoulder Replacement Statistics

Approximately 53,000 people in the United States undergo shoulder replacement surgery each year.[1] This number is increasing at a faster rate than in previous decades, due in part to the introduction of reverse shoulder replacements in November 2003. More than two-thirds of replacements are done in people ages 65 and older, and osteoarthritis is responsible for more than three-quarters of the replacements.[2] The next most common reason is humerus fractures.

of the humerus fits into a shallow socket in the scapula. The socket is called the glenoid, and scientists refer to the joint itself as the glenohumeral joint.

Surgeons can replace just the end of the humerus, or both parts at once. The ball-shaped end of the humerus is replaced with a metal ball anchored to the humerus with a long metal stem. Bone is removed from the humerus and the stem is inserted. The glenoid is replaced with a sturdy plastic socket. Sometimes, a firsthand look at the patient's shoulder is needed to decide whether to replace both parts or just the end of the humerus. The surgeon may make the final decision during the surgery itself.

Patients with severe tearing in the shoulder muscles or those whose previous shoulder replacements have failed may receive what is known as a reverse total shoulder replacement. In this procedure, the ball is attached to

Like knee replacements, shoulder replacement surgeries generally take approximately two hours.

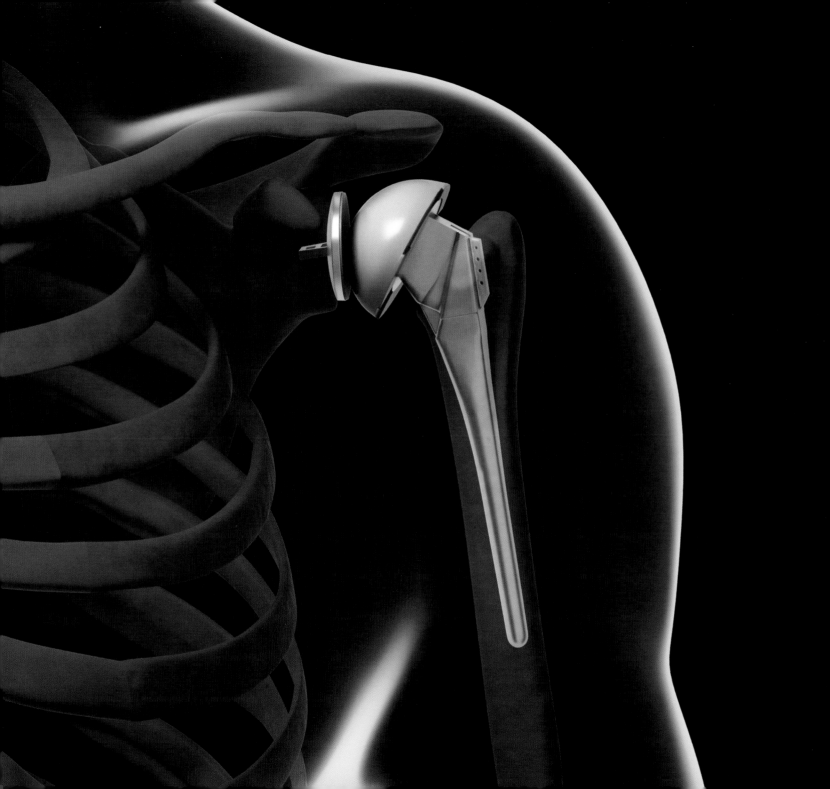

+ Shoulder Resurfacing

For patients who have relatively little damage to their shoulder joint, and especially those who are young, doctors may recommend resurfacing rather than total replacement. In this technique, medically known as resurfacing hemiarthroplasty, the end of the humerus is replaced with a metal ball, without a stem being inserted into the humerus. This minimizes the amount of bone removed from the humerus and also prevents the issues that can come along with the loosening or weakening of a total shoulder replacement. Additionally, the resurfacing procedure can be adapted into a total replacement in the future if needed. Throughout the body, many of the major joints that can be replaced can also be resurfaced as a more conservative approach.

the scapula and the socket is attached to the end of the humerus. This allows the patient to use different muscles to lift his or her arm, since the ones normally used are too damaged to function properly.

When doctors recommend a shoulder replacement, the patient is usually in severe pain as a result of shoulder problems. This pain can happen not only when actively moving the arm but also when simply resting. The pain can be so severe it prevents the patient from sleeping well. If medication and physical therapy do not improve the patient's condition, surgery may be the only option to relieve the pain.

Wrist Replacement

The wrist joint is among the most frequently used joints in everyday life. Writing, opening a door, and petting a dog or cat all require its use. Although the wrist is a relatively small joint, it is more complex than the hip or the knee joint.

A 2011 Norwegian study showed that while the quality of wrist replacements has improved dramatically in recent decades, the life span of wrist joint implants still lags behind those of replacement hips and knees.

At the base of the hand, eight bones, called the carpals, connect with the two bones of the forearm, the radius and ulna. Joints connect the radius to the ulna and the radius to the carpals, allowing a wide range of movements and motions at the wrist. As in the other joints, cartilage and synovial fluid lubricate the joints to permit smooth movement. If these cushioning materials wear away or become damaged due to injury or disease, a painful arthritic condition can arise. Wrist joint replacement may be needed to restore strength in the hand and wrist.

Wrist implants generally consist of two metal parts and a plastic spacer. The first metal part fits into the radius, and the second is secured to the carpals. The plastic spacer fits between the parts. It is designed to glide smoothly on the arm side, while remaining steady on the hand side. This allows for natural hand motions. The size of the plastic spacer is changed based on the size of the patient's hand.

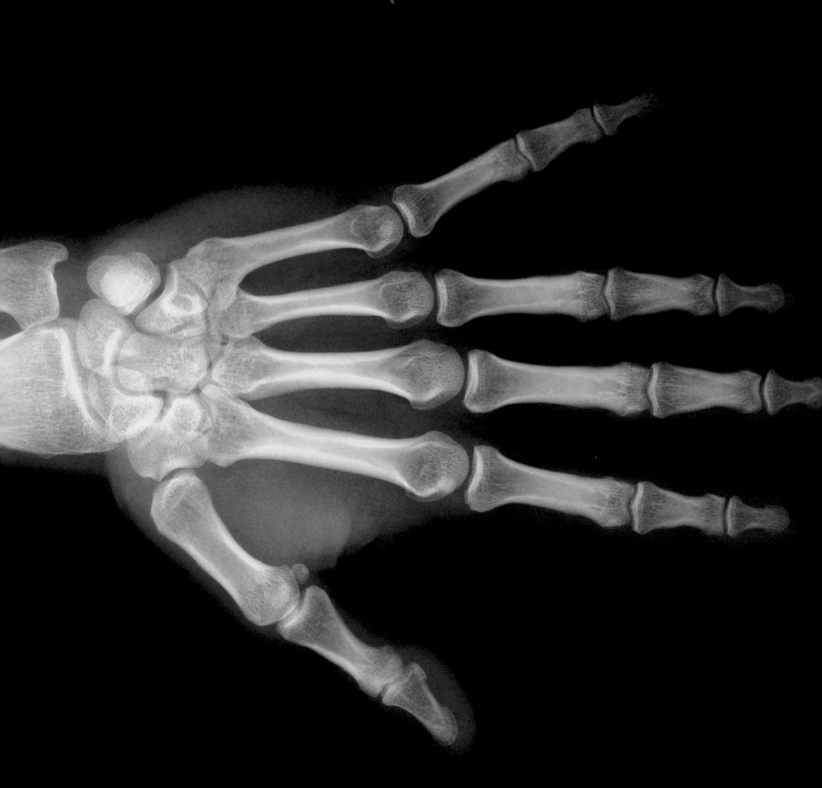

Ankle Replacement

Like the hip and knee joints, the ankle joint is critical in normal walking motions. The joint connects the tibia and fibula with one of the anklebones, called the talus. This connection allows mostly for an up-and-down hinge motion. It works together with other smaller joints lower in the foot to create the complex movements possible during walking. Implants generally connect the tibia and the talus.

Because it supports the weight of nearly the entire body, the forces on the ankle joint can sometimes be greater than those on the knee or hip. Additionally, the contacting surface of the talus itself is very small—only a quarter the size of the patella. This creates a small area for the implants to take hold, whether cemented or uncemented. These factors mean replacement of the ankle joint carries special challenges for surgeons.

Advancing Ankle Replacement Technology

When ankle replacements were introduced in the 1970s, the quality of the implants was poor. "Everybody gave up on them," says Dr. James Brodsky, a Dallas orthopedic surgeon.[3] However, advancing technology has made them more effective and more popular. Approximately 4,400 patients received ankle replacements in 2010.[4] Still, it is less popular than the solution used before the development of ankle replacements. Ankle fusion surgery, in which the joint is removed and the bones are simply screwed together permanently, was done on 25,000 patients in 2009.[5] Though it limits motion, ankle fusion is effective at stopping pain. Modern ankle replacements are getting better, but there is still a risk of them breaking during heavy activity. Also, additional surgeries are usually needed when the implant wears out.

 Due to the complexity and small size of the wrist joint, wrist replacement is sometimes more difficult than knee or hip replacement surgery.

Rare Types of Replacements

Other joints are replaced more rarely. These include a few of the joints in the fingers. The metacarpal-phalangeal (MP) joints—those where the fingers meet the hand—and the distal interphalangeal (DIP) joints—those at the next knuckle—can be replaced. The surgery has been done since the 1950s to restore joint motion, to improve the look and alignment of the joint, and simply to relieve pain. The hands are often among the first parts of the body afflicted with arthritis, making knuckle replacements a natural choice for surgeons. Patients who receive the procedure usually suffer from either rheumatoid arthritis or osteoarthritis. However, doctors typically perform the operation only if pain is severe enough to interfere with daily life and if the patient's hand has lost significant strength.

Finger joint replacement surgery is a relatively quick procedure compared to the replacement of larger joints. Each knuckle takes approximately 30 minutes to replace. However, the recovery can be a long process. Several months of therapy are needed following finger joint replacement to ensure a healthy recovery. Though finger joint replacements are uncommon compared to hip and knee replacements, some doctors believe they could increase in number as the population grows older and more people are afflicted with arthritis.

Toe replacement is a fairly new, cutting-edge technology. Researchers are studying replacements for the joint at the base of the big toe, known as the first metatarsal-phalangeal (MTP) joint. The joint

Because many blood vessels and nerves travel across the finger joint, surgeons must take extra caution when working in the area.

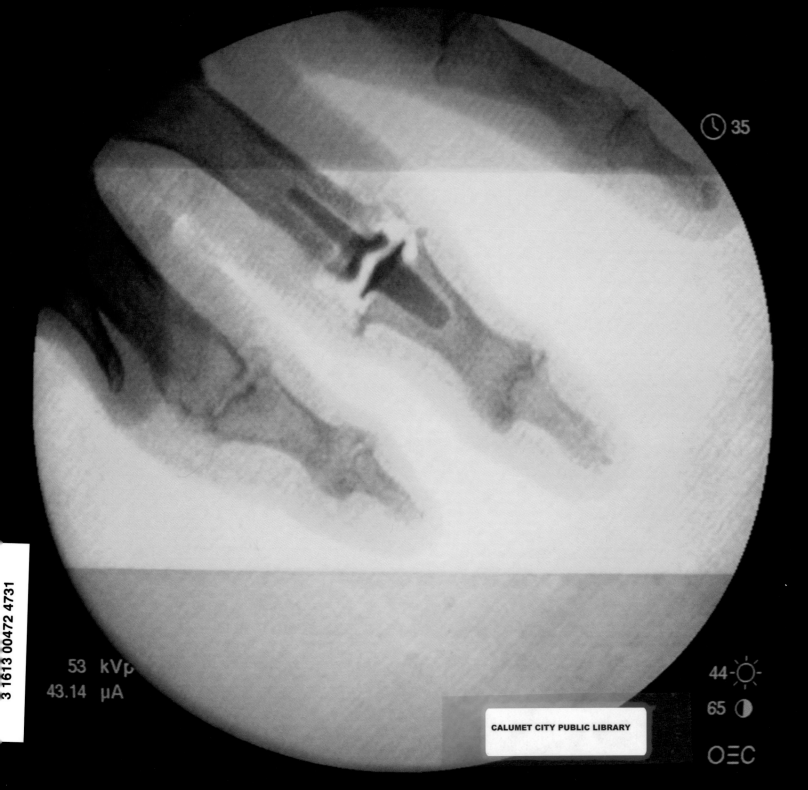

experiences large and complex forces during normal walking motion, making it a challenge to replace. Though replacements have been carried out already, doctors and engineers are working to develop more successful implants for future use.

Elbow replacement, too, is a relatively new procedure. The elbow consists of three separate joints. At the elbow, joints connect the radius and ulna each to the humerus and allow for the elbow's hinge movement. A third joint connects the radius to the ulna, permitting rotation of the forearm. Typical implants consist of two metal stems with a plastic hinge between them. The stems are anchored to the lower end of the humerus and the upper end of the ulna. The plastic hinge allows for the two stems to smoothly move back and forth in a hinge motion.

Elbow replacements require considerable healing time. Patients may have to wait 12 weeks to use their new elbows, and complete recovery may take up to a year.

A patient receives light exercise after undergoing an elbow replacement surgery.

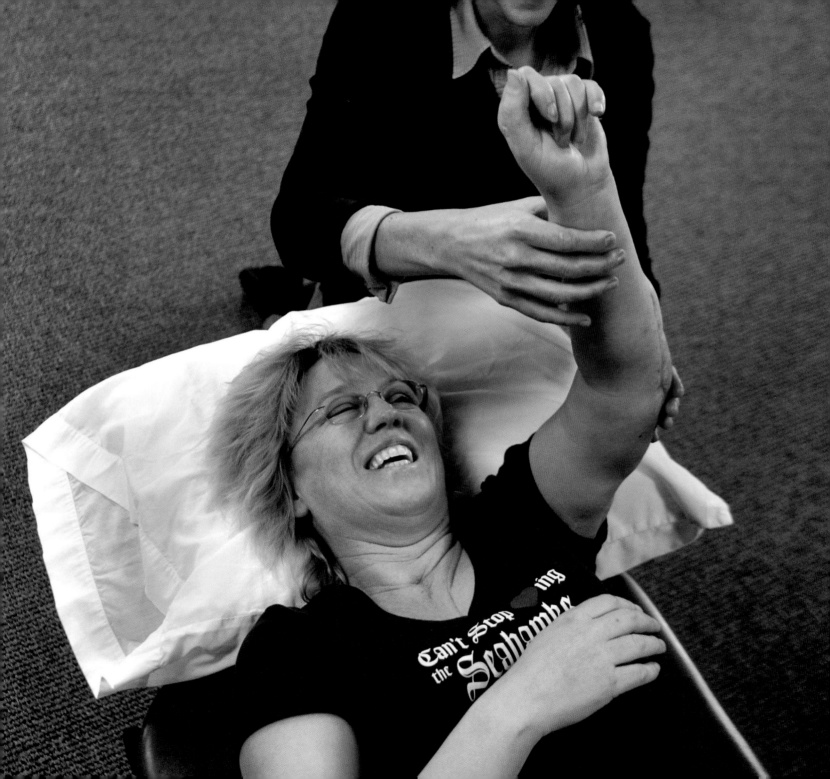

Joint Replacements and Physical Activity

Before the availability of joint replacements, severe arthritis or joint injuries often meant people had to give up the sports they loved playing. But today, joint replacement technology can let patients return to an active, functional lifestyle. Though activity usually needs to be reduced from preoperative levels, the quality-of-life difference joint replacement brings is significant for many active patients.

Surgeons caution heavy exercise can put too much pressure on joint replacements, increasing the chance of them breaking, wearing out, or loosening. But at the same time, moderate exercise can increase the health of the patient and of the tissues surrounding the implant. In uncemented replacements, the implant is designed to promote bone growth. This new bone helps secure the

Famed athlete Bo Jackson was able to return to his baseball career after a 1991 hip replacement.

Activity Recommendations after Hip Replacement

A 1999 survey of surgeons performing total hip replacements asked the surgeons to classify various activities based on whether they would recommend patients return to the activities after surgery. Some activities, such as golf, croquet, and swimming, were recommended outright. Others, including bowling and canoeing, were recommended only if the patient had prior experience. A third group of activities was discouraged completely. These included basketball, football, and hockey.

implant in place. Since exercise can promote improved bone quality and growth, it can help strengthen the connection between existing bone and the implant. Exercise also has benefits for those with cemented replacements, increasing muscle strength, improving coordination, and making it less likely a patient will fall and reinjure the joint.

The preferred activities are those that put less stress on the joints. They include cycling, swimming, and walking. Studies have shown some patients actually increase their participation in low-impact activities after joint replacement surgery, in part to take advantage of exercise's benefits. High-impact activities, such as running or tennis, may be riskier. Heavy wear and tear on the implant may result in the need for another surgery, known as a revision. Because additional remaining bone is scraped away during a revision surgery, there is less and less bone

Because it puts less stress on joints than other activities, cycling is one ideal low-impact activity for joint replacement patients.

Joint Replacements and Weight

If a person is overweight by just 10 pounds (4.5 kg), the force on the knee can be increased by up to 60 pounds (27 kg) each time he or she takes a step.[1] Active individuals who want to hike, run, and play sports will experience even more force on their joints. The more force is imposed on an implant, the more likely it is to wear and fail. This makes a healthy weight one of the most important things for patients to consider when planning a postoperative return to activity.

available each time a revision is carried out. This can make revision surgeries riskier and more complicated.

Returning to an Active Life

Though some patients increase their activity levels after surgery, preoperative participation in a particular sport usually determines whether a patient continues to participate in the sport after surgery. In one study, a majority of patients who played sports before knee replacement surgery continued playing afterward. Many athletic patients assume they will be able to return to their sport at the same level of intensity after a hip or knee replacement. This is generally advised only for patients participating in lighter activities. Studies have shown that participating in high-impact sports results in needing a revision sooner than would otherwise be necessary, particularly in younger patients who are more active to begin with. If patients insist on returning to high-impact sports, surgeons typically inform them of the risks involved.

The approach taken to the surgery can depend on the life story of the patient involved. Firefighter Kenneth Knott was an avid outdoorsman and scuba diver. His first sign of pain in his hips was discomfort when walking. Soon the pain started to interfere with his job. He began depending on fellow workers to take some of his workload because he could not move in the way his job demanded. Eventually, he was diagnosed with osteoarthritis of the hip.

When he found himself barely able to walk, Knott knew he had to have surgery. Because he was young, the conservative approach of left hip resurfacing was the answer, instead of a total joint replacement. This left more of Knott's femur bone intact. If he needs revision surgery in the future, it is still possible to install a total hip replacement implant. Following five weeks of physical therapy, Knott was able to return to his job at full capacity. "I am able to do my job at the level I was prior to the first symptoms. Without this surgery I would not have been able to continue working in the career that I love and providing for the citizens that depend on our services."[2]

Different Types of Replacements and Activities

There are still many unanswered questions when it comes to the relationship between joint replacements and physical activity. Dr. Robert T. Trousdale of Minnesota highlights this fact, saying, "There are really no well-done prospective, randomized activity data that justify the use of certain activities. Hence, I think we are left with using a common-sense approach."[3] In particular, some advanced

A patient, *left*, rides a stationary bicycle following his knee resurfacing surgery.

materials used in new joint resurfacing technologies lack the long-term follow-up studies needed to get a good sense of how well they work for patients over time.

However, there are some general prospects for the ability of patients who have particular joints replaced, or who undergo certain kinds of joint procedures. Opinions about these prospects vary by surgeon. Some surgeons say those who receive hip resurfacing can generally participate in more strenuous activities than most other patients with joint issues. Especially fit patients have even returned to skiing, football, and running. However, it is still unclear how well these patients' resurfaced hips will hold up after several years of these high-impact activities.

With knee replacement surgery, fewer patients are able to successfully return to their sport of choice. Artificial knee

Striking a Balance

Orthopedic surgeon Markus Kuster, a leading researcher into the relationship between joint replacements and physical activity, notes, "There is evidence that a balance exists between too little activity, leading to decreased bone density, and early loosening within 10 years, and too much activity, leading to increased wear and later loosening after 10 years."[4] Striking this balance can give patients the maximum quality of life with their new joint.

> One study showed knee replacement patients walked an average of 640,000 steps per year following their surgery, while hip replacement patients walked an average of 950,000.[5] In 2003, the average American walked approximately 1.87 million steps per year.[6]

joints have not been able to completely duplicate the real knee's ability to twist and turn in the complex ways required for some sports while maintaining the stability, strength, and control of the lost natural structures.

In patients receiving total shoulder and ankle replacements, the stability of the joint can also be an issue. According to one study regarding shoulder replacement, though, a significant number of golfers were able to return to their sport, even improving their game. Such a dramatic recovery requires a long and careful period of rehabilitation following surgery.

Total ankle replacement is still a very new surgery, so few studies have been done to show its effect on physical activity. Until playing sports on an artificial ankle is shown to be safe, studies recommend patients avoid high-impact activities entirely.

Simply being able to return to everyday activities such as gardening can boost the quality of life for joint replacement patients significantly.

Risks of Joint Replacement

As with any kind of surgery, joint replacement surgery has risks. Before the patient goes under the knife, his or her surgeon typically requests a complete physical examination in order to minimize these risks. By getting as much information as possible on the patient, the surgeon will tailor the surgery and recovery procedures to ensure the patient's health. Potential risks of joint replacement surgery include those common to many kinds of surgery, such as infections, an increased risk of heart attack, and problems with bleeding and blood clotting. There are also risks unique to joint replacements—failure of the implanted joints and allergic reactions to the implant materials.

The possibility of having a heart attack is a common risk after any surgery. Increased risk of a heart attack is a result of aftereffects of anesthesia, blood loss, and lack of oxygen. Additionally,

Though joint replacement surgery is considered relatively safe and routine, there are still risks involved with the procedure.

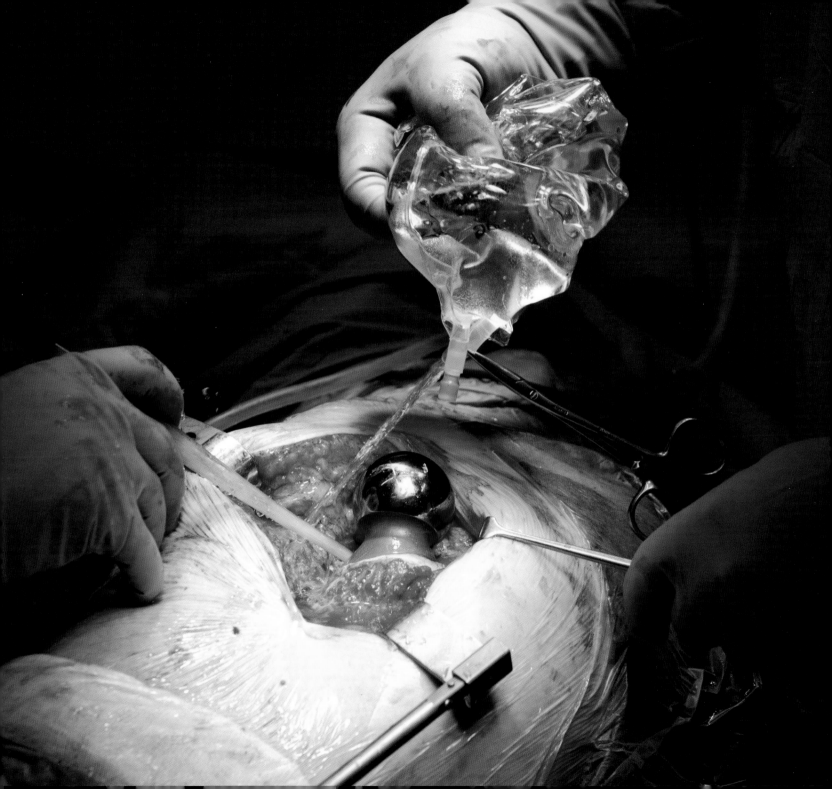

Joint Replacement and Heart Attacks

Although the likelihood of having a heart attack increases dramatically after a joint replacement surgery, it is important to remember the chances of having a heart attack are not very high to begin with. In one study, the number of people who had a heart attack within six weeks of their hip replacement was just one in 200. For those receiving knee replacements, the odds dropped to just one in 500.[2] Compared with the risks following similar surgeries, the heart attack risks of joint replacement are not unusual.

surgery—or even just the thought of it—can be very stressful for patients.

One study has shown in the first two weeks after surgery, the heart attack risk for hip replacement recipients increased to 25 times the normal rate. Knee replacement recipients saw their risk increase by 31 times.[1] However, the researchers also found in the weeks following this initial two-week period, the risk of heart attack dropped. Heart attack risk can be reduced using heart medications and by ensuring the heart is carefully monitored during the recovery period.

Another potential risk is bleeding. It can occur during and following joint replacement surgery. To combat this risk, doctors sometimes recommend the patient have blood drawn before surgery, just in case the patient needs additional blood during the procedure. The patient may also need to stop taking certain medications before surgery, since some medications, such as aspirin and ibuprofen, can promote excessive bleeding.

Bleeding is not the only blood-related risk of joint replacement surgery. Blood clots can also pose a danger. A blood clot is a jellylike mass of thickened blood. Ordinarily, blood clotting is beneficial, stopping bleeding. After hip surgery, there will be a blood clot near the new hip joint, which is normal.

However, blood clots can prove dangerous if they block the normal flow of blood. This can cause pain, tenderness, and swelling of the leg. Even worse, if the clot breaks loose and travels through the bloodstream, it can travel through the heart and block blood flow to the lungs. This results in a pulmonary embolism, leading to chest pain and shortness of breath. If the clot is severe or prolonged, it can be fatal. Anticlotting medicines, compression leggings during surgery, and elevation of the feet can help prevent blood clots following hip replacement surgery.

Another risk of joint replacement surgery is infection. Infection may occur in the incision or around the implant itself. It can happen not only in the hospital, but also at home. The infection can even come years later. Depending on the severity of an infection, the usual methods of treatment are antibiotics, additional surgery, or even removal of the implant.

Approximately one in 100 patients who receive hip or knee replacements will develop an infection.[3] Some people are more at risk of developing infections than others after a joint replacement procedure, especially those with immune system diseases. These people's immune systems are less able to cope with any bacteria that may enter the body during surgery.

Implant Infection

The metal and plastic parts making up artificial joints allow the replacement joint to be both sturdy and flexible. But these same parts also make the implant susceptible to infection. Though the immune system is effective at countering infections in the bloodstream, bacteria sometimes make it onto the implant's surface or find their way inside it. When this happens, it can be difficult for the body to fight off the infection. Surgery is usually needed to cure an infection that gets into implants.

Possible Implant Problems

When an implant stops working, the patient may experience stiff joints and pain may return. Besides the risk of infection, joint replacement surgery can also damage nerves, blood vessels, and bones in the affected area. When these parts are pushed out of the way or cut into when the new joint is installed, they can accidentally be damaged.

One of the most serious postoperative problems that can occur is catastrophic failure of the joint replacement.

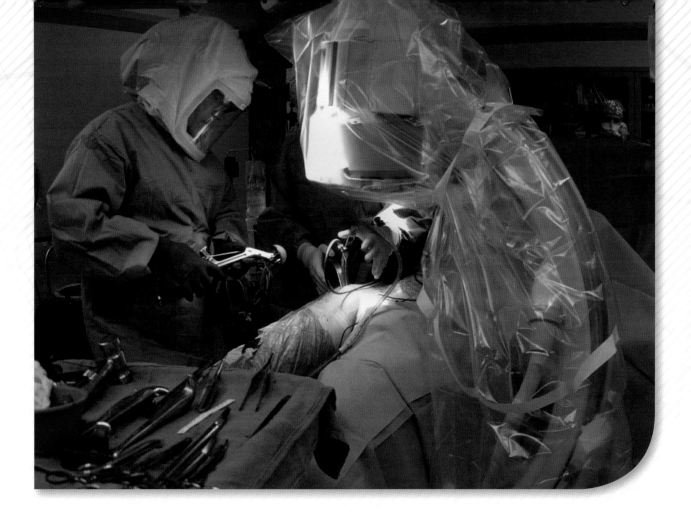

In catastrophic failure, the metal or plastic parts of the implant fracture or otherwise break, usually as a result of excessive force or loosening of the joint's components. It most commonly occurs with knee replacements and is seen less frequently in shoulder and hip implants. Avoiding a catastrophic

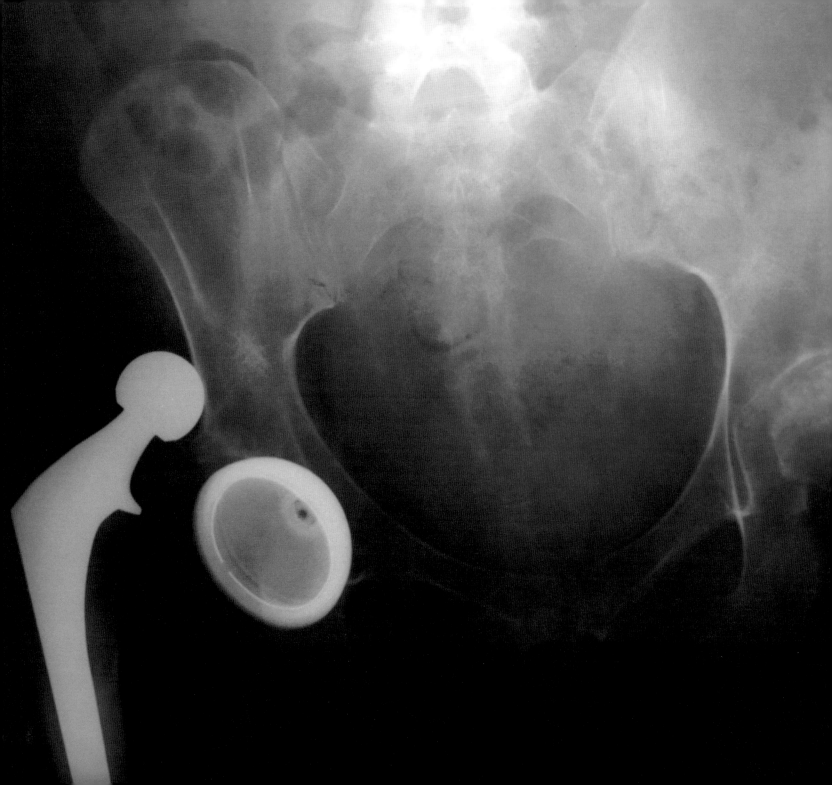

joint replacement failure is typically a matter of limiting oneself to light activity and avoiding high-impact movement.

In March 2012, British experts called for a ban on metal-on-metal hip replacements after data on more than 400,000 artificial hip recipients in the United Kingdom provided "unequivocal evidence" that the devices have a higher than average rate of failure.[4]

There are also risks associated with the materials used in joint replacement. In particular, the metal-on-metal style of implant has become controversial. In this style of replacement joint, metal parts move against other metal parts as the joint moves, rather than one of the points of contact being plastic. The use of metal-on-metal hips has fallen sharply in recent years, but not before thousands malfunctioned well before the devices' expected life expectancies. The failures led to additional surgeries and even some serious complications.

One of the key problems with metal-on-metal joints is that particles of metal can be scraped off as the patient uses the joint. These particles can damage muscles and other tissues near the joint. Partially obscuring the problem is the fact that current tests are not good at detecting the damage these particles cause. Many surgeons believe that the metal-on-metal devices should have been tested further

 When joint replacements loosen, dislocation or failure can occur.

The FDA and Metal-on-Metal Implants

The Food and Drug Administration (FDA) is a US government agency responsible for regulating food, drugs, and medical products to ensure public safety. Under FDA rules, the companies that created the first metal-on-metal artificial hips were not required to test the implants extensively before selling them widely to the public. Additionally, they were not required to conduct follow-up studies to find out how early patients who received the hips fared. As a result of the controversy over the hips' failure rates, in 2011 the FDA ordered five companies making the implants to produce these follow-up studies.

before being implanted in more than 500,000 patients. Dr. Henrik Malchau of Massachusetts has said, "There was not enough data to support their widespread use."[5]

In the early 2000s, metal-on-metal implants were used in one out of every three hip replacements in the United States.[6] A loophole in the Medical Device Amendments of 1976 meant metal-on-metal designs were not subject to as much testing as newer designs. Industry lobbyists successfully convinced the FDA to classify all-metal hips as relatively low-risk implant products. Newer designs, using plastic or ceramic for some parts of the implant, usually last approximately 15 years. In recent years, it has become clear metal-on-metal implants are failing much earlier. By 2013, all-metal designs were used in only 5 percent of all hip replacements.[7]

An attorney responsible for lawsuits against implant manufacturers holds a recalled hip implant linked to metal poisoning.

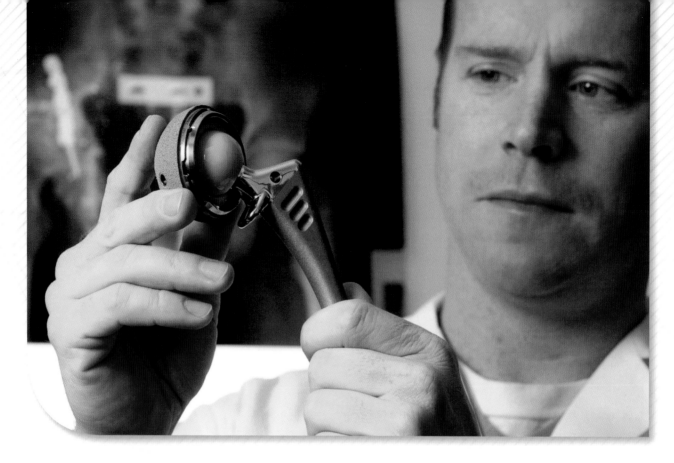

Another potential risk of joint replacement surgery is an allergic reaction to the metal components that make up the implant. Nickel allergies in particular are common in the general population. If nickel is present in an implant inserted into an allergic person, it could lead to swelling, pain, and infection in the joint. Additional surgery is required to remove the implant, clean the area of infection, and insert a new non-nickel implant. One alternate metal commonly used in non-nickel implants is titanium.

In recent years, ceramic hip implants have been associated with more severe squeaking sounds than their metal and plastic counterparts.

Patient age is one major factor in assessing the risks of joint replacement surgery. Young and active people with joint problems may receive resurfacing rather than a full replacement. This procedure, replacing just one component of the natural joint, avoids the risks of wear and tear and loosening that occur in total joint replacements. Most of the all-metal implants used today are used in resurfacing, rather than full replacement procedures.

One rare but potentially serious problem with joint replacements is a squeaking noise when moving the new joint. At first a patient whose new hip squeaks may simply be embarrassed or annoyed at the noise, but some doctors fear the noise is a signal the implant is wearing out. This may lead them to replace the implant sooner than necessary, requiring the risk of a second surgery. The issue has been noticed most prominently in new ceramic hips introduced in the early 2000s.

So far, there have been no reports of squeaking leading to a catastrophic implant failure. But some surgeons are still wary, worrying the shattering of a ceramic implant would leave a huge number of ceramic shards scattered throughout the hip. Patients are also concerned. Dozens have filed lawsuits against hip implant manufacturers, arguing the squeaking in their hips has a negative impact on their quality of life.

7

Recovery

Even when the surgery is over, the process of joint replacement is far from finished. The period after the surgery is a critical time for the patient to recover joint function. How well the patient follows the doctor's recovery instructions will ultimately determine the success of the joint replacement. Patients who fail to heed these instructions may end up with a catastrophic failure of their implant, requiring additional surgery long before the end of the expected life span of their new joint.

In any kind of major surgery, the patient can expect to have stitches or staples along the wound, or there may be a suture beneath the skin on the front of the knee. If one has stitches or staples, these will be removed several weeks after the surgery. A suture under the skin does not need to be

The proper combination of rest, medication, and exercise after joint replacement will result in the quickest recovery and the best overall outcome.

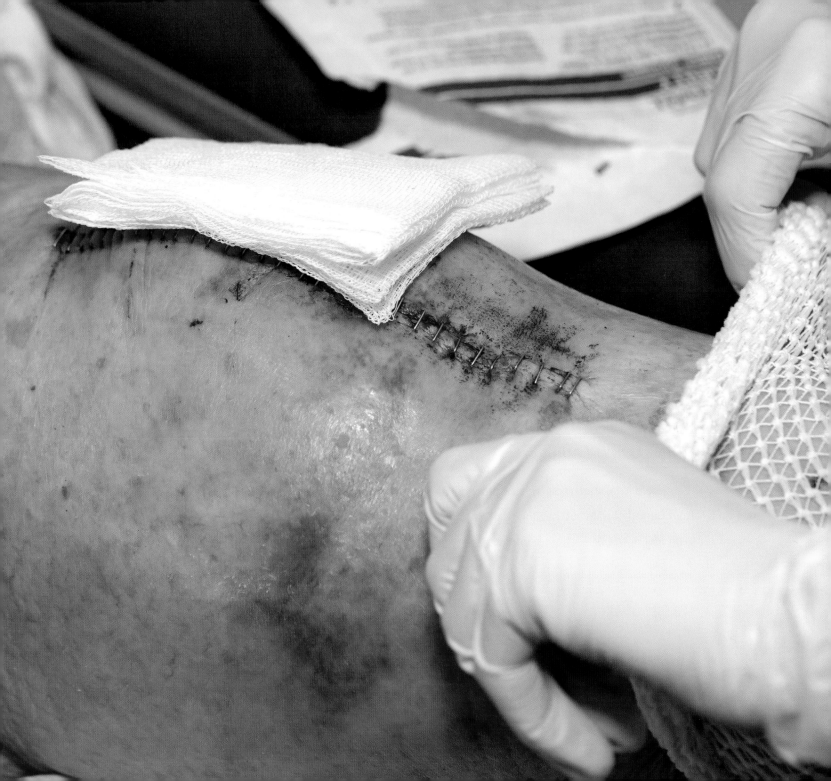

	Knee Replacement	Hip Replacement	Shoulder Replacement	Finger/Wrist Replacement
Recovery Time	3 months	2–4 months	6 months	1–2 months
Implant Life Span	10–20 years	15 years–life	15 years–life	5–15 years[1]

removed. The wound must not be soaked in water until it has completely sealed and dried. It may be bandaged to prevent irritation from clothing.

A patient's diet is a critical part of the healing process following joint replacement surgery. Though the patient can expect some loss of appetite as a result of the surgery, the blood loss caused by the surgery makes a balanced diet even more important. Doctors may also recommend foods high in iron to counter tiredness from blood loss. For the wound to heal properly, and for muscle strength to come back, a balanced diet is important. As always, patients must drink plenty of fluids to keep hydrated and promote the body's healing process.

Because a total knee replacement procedure removes a great deal of bone and tissue, it can lead to a longer period of pain and healing than a hip replacement. With hip replacement surgery, the patient's hips can feel normal after being on crutches for a few months. Total knee replacement surgery, however, can require from six months to one year of patient recovery time due to the inherent instability of the knee joint.

Knee Replacement Recovery

While rest is crucial to a patient's recovery immediately following total knee replacement, the patient will still need to exercise during this time. Exercise can begin as early as the same day as the surgery with the patient's first visit to the physical therapist. Patients begin with light movement to improve blood flow in the leg. Activities are gradually modified and intensified as the patient regains strength and lingering pain decreases.

Before patients can leave the hospital, they must first achieve several benchmarks in knee function. First, they should be able to get in and out of bed without assistance. They should also be able to both bend their knee to a right

Exercise Early and Often

In some ways, the recovery period from joint replacement surgery can begin before the surgery even takes place. Physical therapist Helen Funke says patients should exercise in the time leading up to the surgery: "Try to stay as active as you can tolerate and maintain some form of exercise so you are not deconditioned by the time surgery occurs."[2] It is also important to use caution with pain-relieving medications before surgery. The body can develop a tolerance for the medications, leaving them less effective after the surgery.

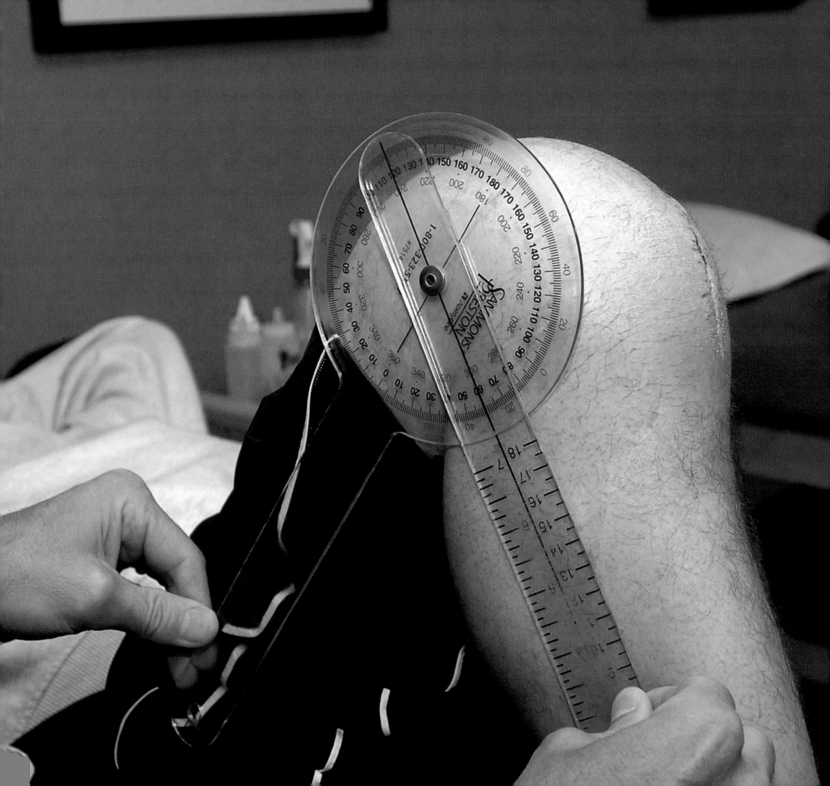

angle and extend it fully. Patients should be able to walk using crutches on flat surfaces and climb a few stairs. Most patients leave the hospital by the end of the first week after surgery.

Doctors recommend that when patients return home, they take precautions to make recovery easier and less risky. Loose carpets and electrical cords should be removed or secured to prevent them from becoming tripping hazards. Furniture can be rearranged to make rooms easier to navigate using crutches and to prevent frequent stair climbing. Patients should also avoid bending over, so doctors may recommend using a grabbing tool to pick up things on the floor.

Several types of activities are helpful after the patient is discharged from the hospital. A graduated walking program is helpful in steadily increasing mobility over time. The program begins with simply walking around the house

Physical Therapy

After joint replacement patients leave the hospital, physical therapy can last up to three months, though some people can reach their goals in less time. Each patient's regimen will be different, owing to the unique nature of each person's surgery, strength, and pain tolerance. One active 54-year-old patient had physical therapy twice daily in the hospital after her knee replacement and left the hospital on crutches after only three days.

A patient's range of knee motion is checked following a knee resurfacing procedure.

before it continues outdoors. It is still important to strike a balance between too little activity and too much. Some patients may unintentionally overdo their recovery exercises, perhaps with the false belief that more activity will result in quicker healing.

If patients drive using their right foot and have their left knee replaced, they can sometimes return to driving just one week after surgery. If their right knee is replaced, six to eight weeks are recommended before driving. Patients typically return to work six to eight weeks after surgery.

Hip Replacement Recovery

After a hip replacement, a physical therapist will visit the patient to explain the capabilities and limitations of his or her new hip. As with knee replacement, light exercise and movement can begin almost right away. By gradually building on this work, patients can maximize the effectiveness of their recovery.

Patients who have received a new hip usually leave the hospital within ten days. Those who go home will require assistance for the weeks following surgery from either a family member or a professional caretaker. They should rearrange furniture and other items in their homes to avoid bending over. Other patients stay at a rehabilitation center as they begin their program of exercise and recovery.

Physical therapists assist a man in a physical therapy exercise during recovery from hip replacement surgery.

Rehabilitation Centers

Major rehabilitation centers provide regularly scheduled physical therapy and round-the-clock access to doctors and therapists. Many focus not just on exercise but also on education of the patient and his or her family. When patients are made aware of nutritional guidelines and the capabilities of their implant, the chances of a successful recovery increase. One large rehabilitation center in New York has patients ranging from young adults to elderly people. On average, its patients stay for one week.

This is more frequently necessary for patients who are elderly or who have other health problems that may slow their recovery.

For patients who go home, doctors recommend setting up a recovery center, a place where they can rest and where anything they might need is within reach. The recovery center is generally centered on a chair with a high seat and a firm cushion. Lower, softer chairs require more effort to pull oneself out of, putting extra stress on the hip. Within reach should be a phone, a walker or crutches, a pitcher of water, books or magazines, and a television remote. Having frozen or prepared meals can also be helpful. Minimizing extra activity and keeping exercise to the doctor's recommended level will help speed the recovery.

Once patients are home, they must carefully monitor signs of potential problems. Doctors recommend they

Mary Ellen, an active knee replacement recipient in her early fifties, is aware of the limitations of her joint replacement. Still, her intense physical regimen makes her confident about her abilities: "I avoid running but could do it if I had to. If I were in danger, I'd be able to get out of the way fast."[3]

take their body temperature twice daily, notifying the hospital if it goes over 100.6 degrees Fahrenheit (38.1°C). Swelling around the hip is likely to continue for up to six months after surgery but can be managed at home by elevating the leg and applying ice. Patients must be especially vigilant for potential blood clots. Shortness of breath and pain in the calves or chest are possible signs of blood clots.

8

The Future of Joint Replacement

Total joint replacement was originally intended to treat the elderly patient population. Today, the population demographics of the 1900s mean more and more people reach age 65 each year, increasing demand from this segment of the population. However, elderly patients are no longer the only focus when it comes to joint replacement surgery. Younger people are increasingly receiving implants. A 2009 study projected that more than half of hip replacements now go to patients younger than 65.[1]

The demographic shift is due in part to changing attitudes. Florida surgeon Mary O'Connor notes, "Younger people are less willing to accept physical disability than older generations. They simply want to remain active. They don't want to hear that they should use a cane or they can't walk or play

A major trend in joint replacements is the emergence of younger patients as candidates for hip and knee implants.

golf or do the activities they want to do."[2] New joint replacement technology means that many patients eager to return to their active lifestyle can do so. Surgeon Kevin Fricka has noted new polyethylene materials used in hip joints are major improvements over older plastic types: "At this point, we have 12 years of data on the new plastic, and it's wearing five to eight times less than old plastics. We should reliably get 15 to 20 years on a replacement, and potentially longer."[3]

Still, no implant today can last forever. Younger patients are likely to require one or more revisions to their joint replacement. Increasing the number of surgeries inherently increases the risks of those surgeries. Additionally, with each revision removing more and more of the patient's original bone, it becomes more difficult to securely anchor new replacements.

Minimally Invasive Surgery

New surgical technologies are making joint replacements easier and more effective. One of the most significant advances has been the development of minimally invasive surgery, also

With the availability of ankle replacement implants and the rapid growth of an aging population, the worldwide ankle replacement market is expected by some to grow from $90 million in 2010 to $400 million in 2015.[4]

Though arthroscopic tools require more surgeon skill, they can provide a large, clear view of the inside of patients' joints.

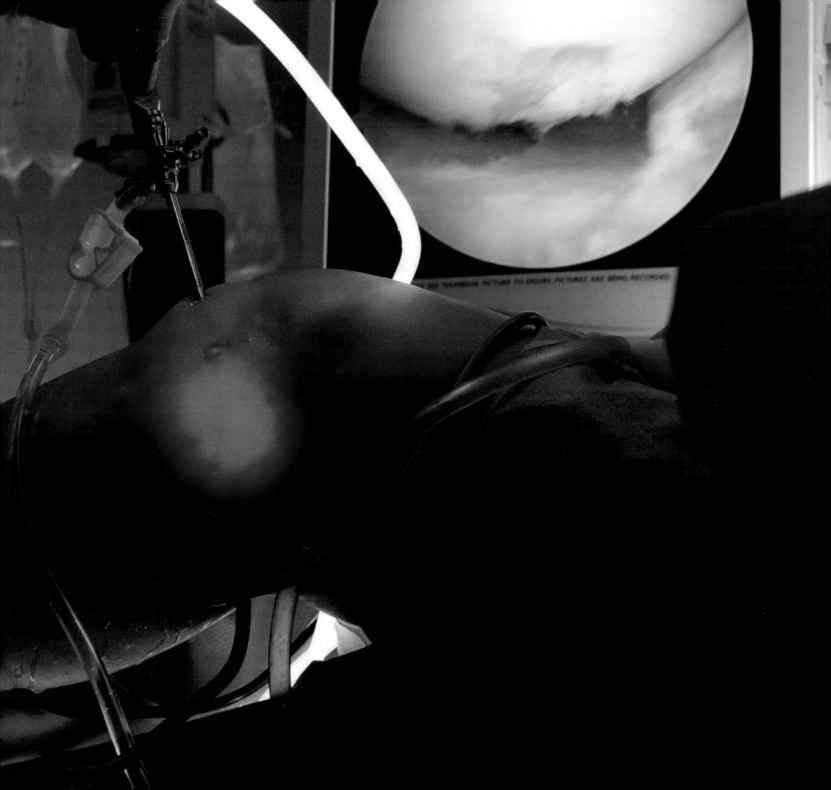

History of Arthroscopy

The first attempts to use a device to look inside a patient's body were made in the late 1800s. The first article on arthroscopy was published in US medical literature in 1925, but the field was not studied further for several decades. Finally, in 1958, a Japanese doctor invented the first successful arthroscope. Seven years later, doctor Robert Jackson brought one of the devices back to his hospital in Toronto, Canada, and began using it. When miniature cameras were invented in the early 1970s, the arthroscope became more popular.

known as arthroscopic surgery. In this technique, the large incisions of standard joint replacements are replaced with relatively small incisions. In the case of hip replacements, the incision is reduced from nine inches (22.9 cm) to as few as three inches (7.6 cm). For knee replacements, the incision can drop from 12 inches (30.5 cm) all the way down to just four inches (10.2 cm).[5] Smaller incisions result in less blood loss and less damage to the surrounding tissue.

Once the incision is made, the surgeon inserts a device called an arthroscope. This is a tube filled with fiber-optic cables and fitted with a source of light. It is often connected to a screen in the operating room. The arthroscope acts as a tiny camera, allowing the surgeon to see the internal structures of the patient without having to make larger incisions. The surgeon can then evaluate how

Inflammation of the knee joint of a person suffering from osteoarthritis is easily visible through an arthroscope.

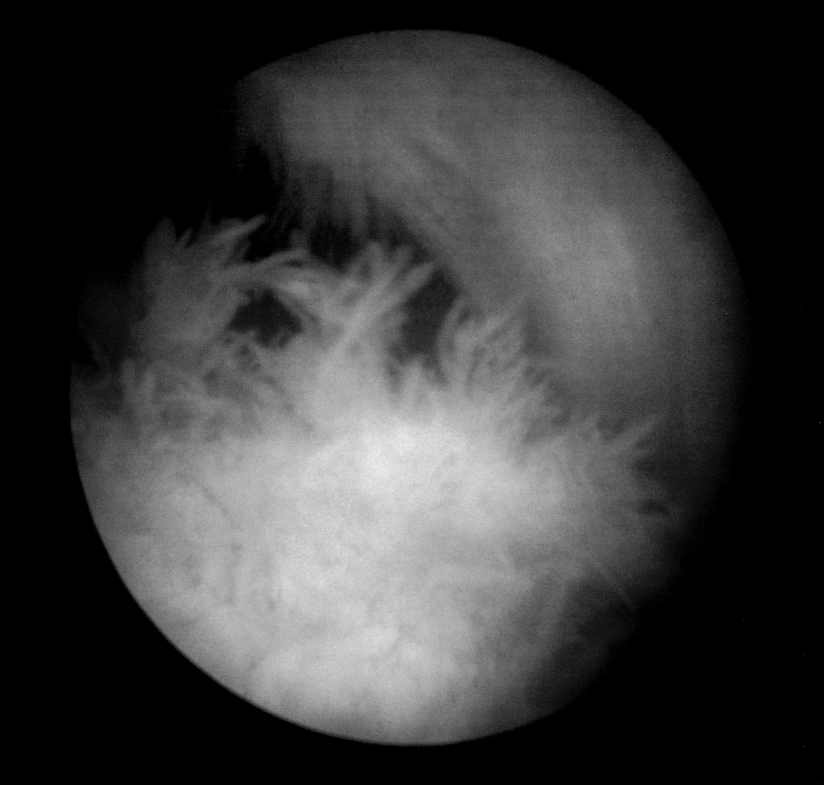

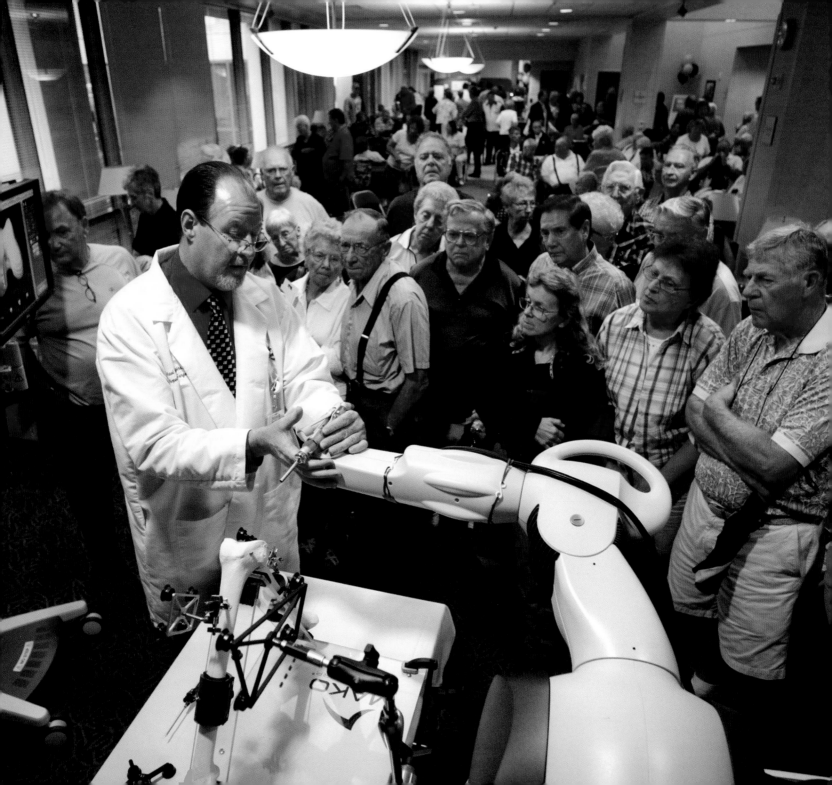

best to proceed. Other arthroscopes, fitted with small tools on the end, are inserted through the small incision to complete the procedure.

Several studies have shown benefits to minimally invasive knee replacement surgery versus traditional methods, including a shorter hospital stay and a quicker recovery. However, other studies have shown a higher rate of complications with minimally invasive knee surgery, including poorer positioning of the knee implants. This has been attributed to the higher surgical skill needed for an arthroscopic procedure. One challenge of minimally invasive surgery is the difficulty of performing the surgery within a restricted visual field. Surgeons cannot get as clear a view of structures through an arthroscope as they could by seeing the entire structure through their own eyes. Smaller tools and specialized techniques mean that only the best surgeons can give patients all the potential benefits of the minimally invasive procedure. Doctors continue studying the effect of minimally invasive procedures as compared with traditional procedures. Infection and dislocation rates, the stability of the new joint, and the precision of the implant positioning are some of the key areas being studied.

Computer-Assisted Surgery

No matter how well trained and educated a surgeon is, he or she is still limited by only having two eyes and two hands. Computer-assisted surgery using robots is one possible way for surgeons to overcome

A doctor demonstrates a robotic arm used to assist with knee resurfacing surgeries.

this barrier. This technology can give the surgeon three-dimensional views of a joint's structure, even when part of the joint is obscured by tissue. It can also improve the quality of joint positioning.

Robots and computers can help guide and support surgeons both before and during the joint replacement. Advanced scanning and manufacturing technologies can create implant parts that are a perfect fit for an individual. During the procedure, special tracking devices measure the exact angles at which the implant is being placed in the body. The computer calculates the correct angle for the implant, and the surgeon makes tiny adjustments to the placement until it is exactly right. In some cases, the surgeon operates a robotic arm rather than making the adjustments by hand, improving the positioning even further. The result of this enhanced accuracy can mean a lower chance of needing a revision surgery.

Still, computer-assisted surgery is not perfect. Though the technique improves joint positioning, it does not completely eliminate the chance of misalignment. Additionally, computer-assisted surgery is so new that long-term studies have not yet been completed. More information will be needed to determine the exact differences between standard surgery and computer-assisted procedures.

A Biological Solution

One vision of the future of joint replacement does not involve metal and plastic implant materials at all. Instead, it uses biological replacements, replacing worn-out parts of joints with parts from other living things. A major proponent of this vision is Dr. Kevin Stone of San Francisco, California.

Stem Cells

Stem cells are undifferentiated cells, meaning they are capable of growing into any kind of cell the body needs. This flexibility has made them attractive to scientists seeking ways to replace cells damaged or destroyed by disease or injury. Some stem cells come from human embryos. The use of these embryos in research has proven politically controversial. However, scientists are studying ways to retrieve stem cells from adult tissues.

At first, Stone used ligaments and cartilage from human donors to replace damaged tissues in joints. He also used patients' own stem cells, human cells that can turn into a wide variety of specialized body cells, to repair and regrow cartilage surfaces in the joints. By repairing the cartilage on the surface of joints, he was able to give patients smoother, less painful motion. However, this technique has a few major limitations preventing it from reaching widespread use. First, the quality and strength of regrown tissues is not always as good as the original tissues. Second, since joint tissue is usually taken from deceased donors, there is not nearly enough to cover the massive demand for joint replacements. Finally, human tissue is extremely expensive, making this solution cost prohibitive.

Stone developed an innovative solution that solved these problems using animal tissue. Animal tissue is relatively inexpensive and plentiful, and he has already demonstrated its quality. Cow tendons have been broken down and re-created into tissue that can be inserted into the human knee to replace damaged tissue. The procedure has been successfully carried out in more than 4,000 patients.[6]

Still, the animal solution created another problem to overcome. Because the tissue is coming from an entirely different organism, the human immune system may attack and reject it. The tissue to be implanted contains antigens, materials that alert the immune system about foreign material entering the body. Ordinarily, the immune system uses this ability to attack bacteria and viruses, but a rejection of the joint tissue could cause the tissue to fail. To fix this problem, Stone and his team developed methods of using acid and other chemicals to wash the tissues of antigens before implanting them. The technique has seen major success, with athletes in high-impact sports returning to their active lifestyles after

Clinical Trials

More than a dozen clinical trials using stem cells to regenerate cartilage are underway or are planned in Norway, Spain, Iran, Malaysia, France, and elsewhere. Scientists have recently identified ways to keep stem cells on track to become cartilage cells, rather than other types. One major potential advantage of stem cells is the possibility of being able to sustain these new cells in a patient for many years.

receiving pig ligament tissue to replace damaged tissue in their joints.

Rising Replacement Rates

One study predicts a dramatic increase in joint replacement rates in the United States over the coming decades. The study looked at projected rates of hip and knee replacements between 2005 and 2030. Its authors estimated the number of hip replacements would grow 174 percent, increasing to 572,000. The number of knee replacements was expected to grow a staggering 673 percent, to 3.48 million procedures.[7] The authors concluded preparations should be made now to train surgeons to meet this future demand.

A Bright Future

Joint replacement technology has come an incredibly long way in the last century. After pioneering researchers like Frank Gunston and John Charnley brought implants into the mainstream, other researchers rapidly built on their work. New materials and techniques have changed joint replacement from an experimental surgery into one of the most common orthopedic surgical procedures in the world.

The result of these advances has been an amazing impact on the quality of life for patients suffering from joint problems. Once forced to resign themselves to a lifetime of pain and restricted movement, millions of people are now able to return to pain-free, active lifestyles. Today, researchers are hard at work inventing the future of

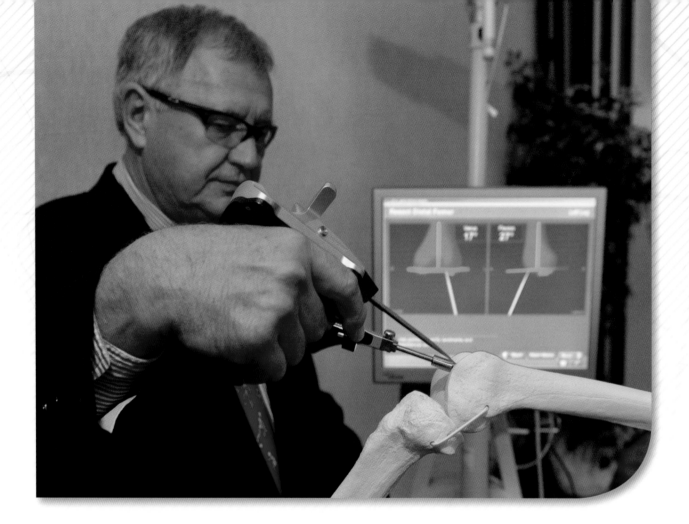

joint replacements. Whether mechanical or biological parts will dominate the future is unclear. However, regardless of the materials used, joint replacement will continue to improve the lives of patients across the globe.

⊕ Timeline

ca. 4500 BCE
Arthritis is first mentioned in writing.

1860s CE
A. B. J. Ferguson develops a technique for inserting cushioning material into the knee joint.

1938
British doctor Phillip Wiles designs a stainless steel artificial hip.

1949
A study in Memphis, Tennessee, shows the poor quality of existing knee replacements.

1950s
Doctors develop the first full knee replacements.

1970s
Ankle replacements are introduced, but the quality of early implants is poor.

1970s
The mobile-bearing knee replacement is developed.

1976
The Medical Device Amendments leave a loophole allowing for lax testing on all-metal implants.

2003
The reverse shoulder replacement surgery is introduced.

2009
A study estimates more than half of hip replacements go to patients under age 65.

1951

Kenneth McKee patents an early hip replacement device.

1954

An article by L. G. P. Shiers lays the groundwork for a new generation of knee replacements.

1958

A Japanese doctor invents the first successful arthroscope.

1962

British surgeon John Charnley develops a successful hip implant.

1968

Surgeon Frank Gunston develops a knee replacement that takes into account the knee's complex motion.

2010

A Swedish study finds that uncemented hip replacements need repair more frequently than cemented replacements.

2011

A Norwegian study finds that wrist replacement quality, while improved, still lags behind the quality of hip and knee replacements.

2011

The FDA orders implant companies to produce follow-up studies on metal-on-metal implants.

2012

British doctors call for a ban on metal-on-metal hip replacements.

2013

All-metal hip replacements drop to being used in only 5 percent of all hip replacements.

✚ Glossary

acupuncture

A procedure involving inserting needles through the skin at specific points to relieve pain or cure disease.

arthroscopic

A surgical method involving the use of smaller incisions and tools than in traditional surgery.

autoimmune disease

A disease in which the body's immune system attacks the body itself.

claustrophobia

The fear of small, enclosed spaces.

collagen

A type of protein that makes up connective tissue in animals and humans.

electromagnet

A magnet created by the flow of electric current.

embolism

The blocking of a blood vessel, usually by a blood clot or a bubble of air.

fusion

The process of permanently attaching two bones.

ibuprofen

A drug used to relieve pain and reduce swelling and reduce fever.

implant

A device surgically placed inside the body.

inflammation

A biological response from the body, often resulting in redness, heat, or swelling of a particular area of the body.

orthopedic

Having to do with the correction of bone and muscle deformities.

revision

A surgery carried out to repair or replace an existing joint replacement.

stem

The part of a joint implant anchored into a carved-out part of the existing bone.

suture

Thread, wire, or other material used to stitch parts of the body together.

synovial

A type of joint that contains lubricating fluid.

Additional Resources

Selected Bibliography

"Joint Replacement." *OrthoInfo*. American Academy of Orthopaedic Surgeons, 2013. Web.

"Knee Replacement." *Mayo Clinic*. Mayo Clinic, 2013. Web.

Further Readings

The Complete Human Body: The Definitive Visual Guide. New York: DK, 2010. Print.

Wood, Elaine, and Pamela Walker. *Understanding the Human Body: The Skeletal and Muscular System*. San Diego, CA: Lucent, 2003. Print.

Web Sites

To learn more about joint replacements, visit ABDO Publishing Company online at **www.abdopublishing.com**. Web sites about joint replacements are featured on our Book Links page. These links are routinely monitored and updated to provide the most current information available.

For More Information

American Academy of Orthopaedic Surgeons

6300 North River Road
Rosemont, IL 60018-4262
847-823-7186
http://www.aaos.org

The American Academy of Orthopaedic Surgeons provides the latest information on advances in joint replacements to both surgeons and patients.

National Institute of Arthritis and Musculoskeletal and Skin Diseases

1 AMS Circle
Bethesda, MD 20892-3675
301-495-4484
http://www.niams.nih.gov

The National Institute of Arthritis and Musculoskeletal and Skin Disorders, one of the US government's National Institutes of Health, is an organization that supports research into joint replacements. It also helps train scientists to conduct this research.

Source Notes

Chapter 1. A Girl Who Lived in Pain

1. Jennifer Davis. "Caitlin Ryan: Tiny Dancer." *Arthritis Today*. Arthritis Foundation, 2013. Web. 10 May 2013.

2. Ibid.

3. Jennifer Davis. "Caitlin Ryan's Top 10 Pain Fighting Tips." *Arthritis Today*. Arthritis Foundation, 2013. Web. 10 May 2013.

4. Jennifer Davis. "Caitlin Ryan: Tiny Dancer." *Arthritis Today*. Arthritis Foundation, 2013. Web. 10 May 2013.

5. Jennifer Davis. "Caitlin Ryan's Top 10 Pain Fighting Tips." *Arthritis Today*. Arthritis Foundation, 2013. Web. 10 May 2013.

6. Jennifer Davis. "Caitlin Ryan: Tiny Dancer." *Arthritis Today*. Arthritis Foundation, 2013. Web. 10 May 2013.

7. Ibid.

Chapter 2. Joints and Joint Problems

1. Paula Rackoff. "Are Men or Women More Likely to Develop Rheumatoid Arthritis, and Why Is That the Case?" *ABC News*. ABC, 18 Nov. 2008. Web. 10 May 2013.

2. "Get the Facts." *Arthritis Foundation*. Arthritis Foundation, 2013. Web. 10 May 2013.

3. Brian Braiker. "Joint Decisions." *Prevention*. MSN Healthy Living, Dec. 2012. Web. 10 May 2013.

Chapter 3. Hip and Knee Replacements

1. Tracey Bryant. "Listen-Up Ladies: Don't Postpone Knee-Replacement Surgery." *UDaily*. University of Delaware, 9 Jan. 2008. Web. 30 May 2013.

2. Nils P. Hailer, Göran Garellick, and Johan Kärrholm. "Uncemented and Cemented Primary Total Hip Arthroplasty in the Swedish Hip Arthroplasty Register." *Acta Orthopaedica* 81.1 (2010). Web. 10 May 2013.

3. B. M. Wroblewski. "Professor John Charnley (1911–1982)." *Rheumatology* 41.7 (2002). Web. 10 May 2013.

4. Jane Elliot. "The Hip History of Joint Replacements." *BBC News*. BBC, 27 Apr. 2006. Web. 10 May 2013.

5. "Total Knee Replacement." *Orthoinfo*. American Academy of Orthopaedic Surgeons, Dec. 2011. Web. 10 May 2013.

6. "Total Hip Replacement." *Orthoinfo*. American Academy of Orthopaedic Surgeons, Dec. 2011. Web. 10 May 2013.

7. Kathryn Smith. "Report: Hip-Replacement Cost Hard to Pin Down." *Politico*. Politico, 12 Feb. 2013. Web. 10 May 2013.

8. L. G. P. Shiers. "Arthroplasty of the Knee." *Journal of Bone and Joint Surgery* 36B.4 (1954). Web. 10 May 2013.

9. Peter Cram, et al. "Total Knee Arthroplasty Volume, Utilization, and Outcomes Among Medicare Beneficiaries, 1991-2010." *Journal of the American Medical Association* 308.12 (2012). Web. 10 May 2013.

Chapter 4. Other Types of Joint Replacements

1. "Shoulder Joint Replacement." *Orthoinfo*. American Academy of Orthopaedic Surgeons, Dec. 2011. Web. 10 May 2013.

2. S. H. Kim, et al. "Increasing Incidence of Shoulder Arthroplasty in the United States." *Journal of Bone and Joint Surgery*. 93.24 (2011). Web. 10 May 2013.

3. Ellyn Couvillion. "Ankles Away." *Advocate*. Capital City Press, 17 Oct. 2012. Web. 10 May 2013.

4. Tara Parker-Pope. "A New Joint Gains as a Candidate for Replacement." *New York Times*. New York Times, 18 Jan. 2010. Web. 10 May 2013.

5. Ibid.

Chapter 5. Joint Replacements and Physical Activity

1. Susan Bartlett. "Role of Body Weight in Osteoarthritis." *Johns Hopkins Arthritis Center*. Johns Hopkins University, 27 Mar. 2012. Web. 10 May 2013.

2. "Patient Story: Hip Resurfacing." *Orthoinfo*. American Academy of Orthopaedic Surgeons, Dec. 2011. Web. 10 May 2013.

3. "Ask the Experts: Advising Patients on Sports Activity Following Joint Arthroplasty." *Orthopedics Today*. Healio, April 2011. Web. 10 May 2013.

4. Marie Westby. "Give Your New Joint a Sporting Chance." *Arthritis Self-Management*. R. A. Rapaport Publishing, 22 Aug. 2012. Web. 10 May 2013.

5. Ibid.

6. Tara Parker-Pope. "The Pedometer Test: Americans Take Fewer Steps." *New York Times*. New York Times, 19 Oct. 2010. Web. 10 May 2013.

Source Notes Continued

Chapter 6. Risks of Joint Replacement

1. Steven Reinberg. "Joint Replacement Boosts Heart Attack Risk Right After Surgery: Study." *Health Day*. US News & World Report, 23 July 2012. Web. 10 May 2013.

2. Daniel Pendrick. "Increase in Heart Attack Risk after Joint Surgery Low but Persistent." *Harvard Health Blog*. Harvard Medical School, 30 July 2012. Web. 13 May 2013.

3. "Joint Replacement Infection." *Orthoinfo*. American Academy of Orthopaedic Surgeons, Dec. 2011. Web. 10 May 2013.

4. "FDA Panel: No Reason to Use Metal-on-Metal Hip Replacements." *Drug Watch*. Drug Watch, 12 Apr. 2013. Web. 13 May 2013.

5. Barry Meier. "FDA Hearing to Focus on Replacement Hips." *New York Times*. New York Times, 26 June 2012. Web. 13 May 2013.

6. Barry Meier. "FDA Seeks to Tighten Regulation of All-Metal Hip Implants." *New York Times*. New York Times, 16 Jan. 2013. Web. 13 May 2013.

7. Ibid.

Chapter 7. Recovery

1. William Hageman. "Cost, Longevity, and Recovery for Replacement Body Parts." *Chicago Tribune*. Chicago Tribune, 27 July 2011. Web. 13 May 2013.

2. Brittany Sozak. "Recovering From Total Joint Replacement Surgery." *Orthogate*. Orthogate, 13 Jan. 2011. Web. 13 May 2013.

3. Brian Braiker. "Joint Decisions." *Prevention*. MSN Healthy Living, Dec. 2012. Web. 10 May 2013.

Chapter 8. The Future of Joint Replacement

1. Jennifer Davis. "Studies Detail Best Hip Replacement Options for Younger Patients." *Arthritis Today*. Arthritis Foundation, 2013. Web. 13 May 2013.

2. Eric Niiler. "As Joint Replacements Grow More Popular, Younger Patients Face Repeat Surgeries." *Washington Post*. Washington Post, 3 Jan. 2011. Web. 13 May 2013.

3. Ibid.

4. Anthony G. Viscogliosi. "The Next Big Thing: Opportunities and Innovations in Total Ankle Arthroplasty." *MDDI*. MDDI, 1 Jan. 2011. Web. 13 May 2013.

5. "Minimally Invasive Surgery for Joint Replacement (Arthroplasty) - A Perspective for Patients." *Hospital for Special Surgery*. Hospital for Special Surgery, 12 Oct. 2009. Web. 13 May 2013.

6. "Kevin Stone: The Bio-Future of Joint Replacement." *TED*. TED, July 2010. Web. 13 May 2013.

7. Steven Kurtz, et al. "Projections of Primary and Revision Hip and Knee Arthroplasty in the United States from 2005 to 2030." *Journal of Bone and Joint Surgery* 89.4 (2007). Web. 13 May 2013.

Index

✚ About the Author

Leslie Galliker is a former newspaper reporter, as well as a former medical transcriptionist. Recently retired, she spends her time writing, pet sitting, visiting children and grandchildren, and being owned by a cat who is quite spoiled. She has been published in magazines and in an anthology.

✚ About the Consultant

Dr. DesJardins is an assistant professor in Bioengineering at Clemson University and leads the two laboratories that focus on biomechanics and orthopedic implant design. He has received engineering degrees from Carnegie Mellon University, the University of Pittsburgh, and Clemson University, and he has worked in research positions at the University of Pennsylvania, Johns Hopkins University, and University College London. He is an active educator in biomedical device design and actively engages in engineering outreach for K–12 students. He founded and codirects the Clemson University Retrieval of Explants Program and Registry in Orthopaedics (CU-REPRO), which is a regional repository that collects and studies retrieved total joint replacement implants. He lives in Clemson, South Carolina, with his wife, Katy Rashid, and their two sons, Rowan and Liam.